TELEVISION
SOAPS

TELEVISION
SOAPS

RICHARD KILBORN

Series Editor: John Izod, Department of Film and
Media Studies, University of Stirling

B. T. Batsford Ltd, London

62150

© Richard Kilborn 1992

First published 1992

Typeset by Servis Filmsetting Ltd, Manchester
and printed and bound in Great Britain
by BPCC Hazells Ltd
Member of BPCC Ltd
for the publishers B. T. Batsford Ltd
4 Fitzhardinge Street, London W1H 0AH

ISBN 0 7134 6509 3

A CIP catalogue record for this book
is available from the British Library

CONTENTS

Dedicated to my parents

ACKNOWLEDGEMENTS

The author would like to acknowledge the assistance of the following: Granada Television; Scottish Television; Yorkshire Television; The BFI Television Stills Library; British Satellite Broadcasting; BBC Television; Radio Times; The Kobal Collection.

A particular thanks to my colleagues at the University of Stirling for their advice and encouragement, and to staff at Scottish Television for always responding promptly to my requests and inquiries.

Studying Soaps

The broad aim of this introductory volume is to explore television soap opera from a number of different perspectives in an attempt to throw light on what is a major broadcasting and cultural phenomenon. About the popularity of television soaps there can be no doubt. As a topic of everyday conversation in home, office or classroom, talk about the latest twist in a story-line or a momentous event in the life of a well-known soap character provides a rich source for constant and enthusiastic conjecture. Many reasons have been advanced to explain the continuing – and some would say rather alarming – fascination that soaps have for such a large number, but one of the most persuasive is that they allow particularly strong bonds to develop between characters and audience. As we shall see when we come to consider the question of the 'reality' of soaps (see Chapter 5), these bonds sometimes become so strong that some viewers feel personally implicated in what happens in the lives of these characters; to the extent that an attempt by the production team to kill off certain characters is often met with vigorous audience protest. What seems to happen is that over a period of time viewers regard soap characters, or even the whole programme, as having moved into the public domain.

Popular myths about soaps

Various explanations have been offered for the tenacity with which viewers cling to or identify with characters in soaps. One of those frequently advanced is that audiences find it possible to relate to these fictional creations in ways often denied them in their real-life relationships. It is almost as if – in an age where an increasing number of people have lost that sustaining sense of belonging to a community, a neighbourhood or even a family group – the possibility of regular involvement in the lives and affairs of a fictional group or community can be a very attractive one. Psychologists might even claim that such an ongoing attachment can be positively beneficial, as it fulfils a compensatory function!

In spite of the evident pleasure which soaps bring to so many viewers on such a regular basis, there have been no small number of people who have been only too ready to pour scorn on what they see as a highly dubious phenomenon. Such critics regard soaps as representing some of the worst excesses of popular television and take exception to what they perceive to be a particularly addictive and mindless form of entertainment. For those who take this view, soaps are simply a waste of time, mere 'chewing gum for the eyes', not particularly offensive in themselves, but guilty of diverting viewers from more challenging and intellectually stimulating types of cultural activity.

In addition to those who take this frankly élitist approach, there are others who believe that soaps can be a positively harmful, if not corrupting, influence. Consumers of certain soaps will – according to these self-appointed moral watchdogs – be tempted to model their own behaviour on the words and deeds of some of the fictional characters they regularly encounter. The argument is that since what is heard and seen in soaps often falls far short of being exemplary or inspiring, who can be surprised if we witness in real life an increasing amount of violent and anti-social, if not downright criminal, behaviour.

Small wonder – in view of the generally low esteem in which soaps are held – that over the years a number of quite potent myths have emerged about what watching too many soaps can do to you. People have been made to feel that a long-term commitment to their favourite soap was equivalent to a dangerous addiction. The result has been that for some viewers an innocent and pleasurable activity, in which there is a high degree of emotional involvement, has become tinged with distinctly guilty feelings. As a consequence of this, many people have not always felt able to admit the pleasures they gain from soaps, for fear that friends and neighbours would think less of them for wasting their time on such trivia.

The pleasures of soap watching

Acknowledging that you are an ardent follower of a particular soap may therefore be something that is not undertaken lightly. At times it even led to what some have referred to as 'covert soap-watching'! This phenomenon is nowadays probably less widespread than it once was, but that it still exists is illustrated from the following lines of a letter, in which a couple enthuse about the fact that there are now three episodes of *Coronation Street* for them to watch each week (there were previously only two).

> We are enjoying the extra evening with *Coronation Street*. It is getting quite exciting! Although we still can't bring ourselves to mention this to our neighbours (you know who!).

Soap weddings become national events

Audience response to soaps

One of the factors which has led to the emergence of these myths
about soaps and soap-watching has been that for far too long whole
series of assumptions have been made about how viewers actually
consume or respond to soaps. Critics – with various axes to grind –
were forever pronouncing on what they presumed to be the prob-
able impact of soaps, without systematically collecting evidence
from the viewers themselves. Research and surveys conducted in the
last few years, however, have thrown a good deal of light on how
audiences actually respond to, or make sense of, the soaps which
regularly command their attention (see Chapter 4). To many readers
it will probably come as no surprise to learn that what all these
surveys point to is the considerable diversity in audience response
both in the degree of involvement in the narrative and in the level of
credibility attached to the various ongoing sagas (Allen, 1985; Morley, 1986 and Taylor and Mullan, 1987). The importance of adopting a reader – or audience-oriented approach to the study of soaps
can thus not be emphasized strongly enough. Only in this way can
one begin to dispel some of the more extravagant claims about a
largely passive, couch-potato audience and reach a better understanding of the types of pleasure to which soaps give access.

Attempting to pinpoint the particular pleasures which soap-
watching can provide is not an easy task, but based on the findings
of the viewer surveys referred to above, one can begin to establish
certain broad categories. First, and possibly foremost, there is the
pleasure of continuing involvement, the anticipation that at a set
time and on a regular basis one will be invited into a world about
which one has acquired – often over a long period of time – a
considerable fund of knowledge. As the late Sir John Betjeman said,
in a much quoted remark about his twice-weekly visit to *Coronation
Street*: 'Mondays and Wednesdays, I live for them. Thank God, half
past seven tonight and I shall be in paradise.' (Nown, 1985, p. 7).
Paradise or not, the contours of the soap opera world become in
many ways as familiar as those which constitute one's everyday
reality. The characters who play major roles in this fictional world
are thus able to become the equivalent of friends or acquaintances.
In fact some viewers will conduct imaginary conversations with
these characters at times when they need comfort or advice, or even
resort to writing to them when the character needs to be warned
that something untoward is about to happen. All this is further
proof of the extent to which soaps can tap into people's imaginative
and emotional lives and of the vicarious pleasure or pain which
viewers can experience as a result of their long-term involvement
with characters.

If one of the pleasures of soap watching derives from a strong sense of involvement, a further source of enjoyment is the endless speculation which a serial encourages amongst its followers. Most fictional narratives are organized in order to promote feelings of expectation or tension, but soaps are particularly adept at stimulating many forms of conjecture. How will a character respond when he or she is given a piece of news to which we, as viewers, are already privy? How long will it be before the character X finds out about Y's infidelity? And what chance does Z have of ever fully recovering from that blow on the head which has led to such severe amnesia? Questions such as these form recurrent components of soap narratives and are at the very heart of soaps' continuing fascination. The promise that next week's episode will go some way towards resolving these uncertainties is part of the unwritten contract between producer and audience, but the pleasure for viewers lies in anticipating just how a character might be manoeuvred out of – or further into – the crisis which looms.

Friends and acquaintances: the *Coronation Street* family (Granada Television)

Individual viewers obviously take great delight in playing through in their mind what developments are likely, given all that has gone before. Quite often, however, these thoughts will not be confined to private musings, but will – as we have already remarked – be talked over in families or among friends. All attempts therefore to analyse the reception of soaps must acknowledge the importance of 'soap talk', principally because it gives the lie to some people's belief that the audience for soaps consists of an undifferentiated mass of passive consumers. Viewers may well become absorbed in these continuing dramas, but this does not mean to say that this is not a critical involvement. Opinions are constantly being expressed, for instance, about various ways in which a soap is not living up to expectations. A story-line may be considered to be decidedly limp or some twist in the narrative wholly implausible. Particular offence is taken at any errors in continuity, when for instance a recent development in a character's life does not square with what is known about his/her past. Dissatisfaction about such lapses is expressed in no uncertain terms, not just to fellow viewers, but also in the form of complaints to the broadcasters themselves (sometimes threatening to take the ultimate sanction of transferring allegiance to a rival soap!).

In short, what emerges from audience response is that – contrary to many of the myths which circulate – viewers often display a considerable degree of sophistication in their 'reading' of soaps. Their relationship to soaps is as much interactive as it is reactive. Nevertheless, in spite of all the skills and knowledge which viewers bring to bear (in terms of viewing-time alone this can represent literally hundreds of hours invested in a programme), audiences have comparatively little power or control – at least in any direct sense – in determining a soap's development. Many letters are received by broadcasters and production teams with suggestions as to how, say, a story-line or character might be developed, but it is only very rarely that any of these ideas are actually used.

A new type of drama serial

Given many viewers' desire for a more active form of involvement in a programme which they consider as much theirs as the property of the production company, it was perhaps only a matter of time before a new type of TV drama serial was devised which allowed for a much greater measure of audience participation than with traditional soaps. In the spring of 1989, Yorkshire Television launched a new programme called *Hollywood Sports*, which the company described as 'the world's first interactive soap opera'. It was intended that *Hollywood Sports* should be an experiment in television democracy and that all those viewers who had hitherto been thwarted in their attempts to influence producers and executives would now for the first time genuinely be able to determine how the various story-lines developed. With regard to the actual type of stories and characters introduced, *Hollywood Sports* was like any other soap. The interactive, democratic element came in when, after the weekly screening of the programme, members of the audience were asked to phone in and give their views as to how the story-lines and characters presently 'in play' should be developed in future episodes. Each of the twenty-minute episodes had a slot built into it for the presentation of two or three alternative plot developments and an on-screen link-person or narrator was on hand to keep viewers up to date with what had already been decided and to explain what options were currently on offer. Later that same evening, after viewers had had the chance to mull over which of the options carried the richest narrative potential and had cast their vote (via an automated soap vote line), the winning option was announced. Viewers were also invited to contribute ideas as to how the various options could be worked up in suitably dramatic form and to even try their hand at producing an actual script.

Though *Hollywood Sports* was discontinued after its initial trial run of twenty weeks, those responsible for the programme declared themselves well pleased with the results of their experiment. To all those involved in the collaborative production process it did of course present a major challenge, since the viewer-originated ideas had to be translated into a viable shooting script and then into a twenty-minute programme against much tighter deadlines than would have been the case with a normal soap production. The fact, however, that *Hollywood Sports* was made to work was significant in more than one respect. Not only did it prove that viewer-driven or 'do-it-youself' TV serial drama was in fact a feasible proposition (television companies in America have since acquired the format rights for the programme), it also showed – by the quantity and quality of scripts and ideas submitted – that a large section of the viewing public had a highly-developed awareness of the rules and conventions according to which soaps operate and the various strategies by which an audience can be hooked and its interest maintained.

That so many viewers wanted and were able to participate in the *Hollywood Sports* experiment is further proof – if any more were needed – that soap watching does not lead to an inevitable dulling of the critical faculties. Indeed, for no small number of viewers it might even be claimed that one of the pleasures of soap watching consists in matching their own knowledge and skills against those of the team professionally concerned with producing the programme material. The sort of pleasures that such viewers derive from following soaps is of the same order as the enjoyment experienced by players of certain types of board game. Moves are made according to a set of agreed rules, which not only govern matters such as plot and character motivation but also the way in which transitions are effected between scenes or how individual episodes are temporarily rounded off. These rules constitute the basic conventions of the soap opera genre, though within the framework of these rules there are practically limitless possibilities as to how individual story-lines and characters can be developed.

The special appeal of soaps

If one thinks of the relationship between soaps and their audience in this light, the pleasures that soap watching afford have a lot to do with how adept the viewer is at spotting the clues or reading the signs which suggest, say, a change in fortunes for a character or prepare viewers in some other way for a significant twist in the narrative. The ability to read the signs in this way naturally presupposes a familiarity with the standard conventions by which soaps operate, together with more than a passing knowledge of the soap in question. Sometimes, of course, even the most skilled 'readers' will be left uncertain as to what significance to attribute to a verbal or a visual clue. At other times audiences are led by the nose into thinking one thing, only in order to increase the element of surprise when the opposite transpires.

Playing with an audience's expectations in this way is in itself a feature of many types of narrative fiction, but with soap opera the teasing component is often quite pronounced. It presupposes a knowing relationship, if not binding contract, between viewer and programme maker as to the nature of what is being offered and how it is presented. For the viewers there is the acknowledgement that in exchange for temporarily (and in the case of soaps regularly) suspending their disbelief, they will be rewarded with an entertaining and absorbing experience. Part of the enjoyment, for some, will be the opportunity of participating in an elaborate guessing game as to which of several available routes the narrative will take. For the production team there is a commitment to structure the entertainment in such a way that it conforms to an established set of consumer expectations without becoming so predictable as to forfeit audience interest or involvement.

In whatever terms one sees the relationship between the soap audience and the programme makers, it is clear that all parties have a considerable amount invested in the continuing success of the enterprise. For the viewer there is – as we have already noted – the awareness that the regular consumption of their chosen soap represents an important viewing commitment which has literally become a part of their lives. (It is doubtless viewers' long-term involvement which leads to worries about what influence soaps have on the formation of attitudes.) For the television company or organization responsible for originating the material, soaps represent a different sort of investment, one that is measured principally in economic terms. Let us therefore consider some of the implications of producing soaps from the company point of view.

The economics of soap production

The principle significance of soaps from the point of view of broadcasters and producers has a lot to do with the programmes' amazing popularity. And unlike certain other types of television programming, this popularity is often not just confined to the domestic market but extends to many countries all over the world. (For more details of soaps as an international phenomenon see Chapter 6.) The considerable potential income from export sales can therefore often be part of the economic calculation in the initial decision to commit resources to the production of a continuing drama. In other words: though the start-up costs for a new soap production can be quite considerable, there are also good prospects for a healthy return on this initial investment. One only needs to look to the Lorimar company in the United States and the Grundy organization in Australia to see what large profits can be made from a continuing involvement in soap opera production.

Whether or not the broadcasters produce their own drama programmes or screen bought-in material, most soap operas have established themselves as trusty 'bankers' so far as generating high audience ratings is concerned. Even relatively low-budget productions can sometimes be remarkably successful if they succeed in becoming a cult phenomenon with more specialist audiences. For the companies operating in the independent/commercial sector, this means that a premium rate can be charged for advertising in the slots before, during and immediately after the screening of a popular soap. In this respect soaps play a significant role in ensuring that the flow of advertising revenue – the economic life-blood of the independent/commercial operation – is maximized.

A further – and related – advantage for the television companies involved in the production of soap operas is that a successful soap can provide a solid economic base on which to build a range of

Take the High Road

DRAMA
500 × 30' (continuing in production)
625 Line PAL Video Tape
1" C-Format, or 2"

This series tells the story of everyday life in a West Highland village in the 1980's.

Glendarroch Estate, and the village that shares its name, are situated in the West of Scotland, somewhere north of Glasgow. It is a tight knit community where the folk live a hard life by present day standards, but Glendarroch and its people are not cut off from the problems and pressures of the modern world.

Although there are over 500 episodes, natural breaks in the story line mean that a commitment to the whole series is not necessary.

"Take the High Road" stars **Edith McArthur, Eileen McCallum, Kenneth Watson, Alec Monteath** and **Caroline Ashley.**

Producer: Brian Mahoney
Executive Producer: Robert Love

All enquiries to:
Michael Trotter
Head of Programme Sales
Scottish Television International
Cowcaddens, Glasgow G2 3PR
Telephone: 041 332 9999
Telex: 777087

SCOTTISH TELEVISION
INTERNATIONAL

other programmes. One might cite here the example of Britain's longest-running television serial *Coronation Street*. In the three decades of its existence the programme has consistently been at or near the top of the television ratings and has brought for its producers, Granada Television, a worldwide reputation. The success of the programme has not only enabled the company to launch a series of merchandising and promotional ventures, but it has also drawn attention to Granada as a provider of 'quality popular programming.' This in turn has enabled the company to become involved in other forms of programme production, in the sphere of both drama and current affairs, which have further reinforced its reputation.

Furthermore, *Coronation Street*, because it is rooted in a definably Northern setting, can still for certain purposes be considered an identifiably 'local' programme. So, bearing in mind that one of the requirements which the Independent Broadcasting Authority (now replaced by the Independent Television Commission) has made of its franchise holders is that a proportion of their programming should reflect a sense of regional identity, Granada, over the years, have been able to parade *Coronation Street* as a classic example of the regional type. The programme thus serves an additional valuable economic function in that it can be used to persuade the IBA that Granada have more than earned the right to continue as a major provider of both local and network programming. Sometimes of course it is possible that a television soap becomes almost too closely identified with a particular company. A case in point was Yorkshire Television's popular 'rural' soap *Emmerdale*. In a recent publicity campaign for their programmes, viewers were reminded that there is more to Yorkshire's output than the twice-weekly story of Northern farming folk!

Since television soaps are one of the most reliable means of attracting a loyal, multi-million audience, considerable attention is paid to the way they are scheduled. For one thing, the audience for a successful drama serial may be persuaded to stay on for further programmes the channel has to offer (the so-called channel loyalty factor). For another, a shrewdly scheduled soap opera can have the highly desirable effect of luring viewers away from watching a programme put out by a rival channel.

In the increasingly competitive world of television it seems inevitable that scheduling will play an even more vital role than hitherto and that soaps – for the reasons already advanced – will remain one

The importance of international sales, *Take the High Road* (Scottish Television)

A scene from *Emmerdale* (Yorkshire Television)

of the major instruments for capturing and maintaining viewer attention.[1] This is not to suggest that those entrusted with the task of scheduling have free rein in deciding at what point in the day's or night's offerings to insert the programme in question. Almost invariably, television serials have been made with a particular family audience in mind, which means in effect that most soaps occupy the daytime or early evening slots, in order to be able to access the largest possible number of viewers. The corollary of this is that most soaps have to be duly circumspect in the way they treat certain issues in order to remain within the guide-lines of what is considered to be family entertainment. All human life has to be there, but 'filtered' in such a way as to cause the least possible offence (see pp. 96–8).

---

1   If anything, the task of the scheduler will become more crucial than it once was, as viewers will have access to more channels (both terrestrial and satellite). Patterns of viewing are also changing as a result of more individuals having a TV set in their own room and of the growing use of video recorders for time-shifting purposes.

From the company or institutional point of view, soaps have the added attraction that in many cases they can be produced at comparatively low cost after start-up expenditure has been met. One has to add the qualification 'in many cases', since with soaps belonging to the 'supersoap' category the costs can be formidable, though here again, even these costs only constitute a small fraction of the profits made from national and international sales. By contrast, production costs for the less glitzy television serials, – which for the sake of convenience we shall categorize as 'traditional' – can be considerably lower than for other types of television drama.

The reasons for this are not difficult to gauge. Soaps, almost by definition, will focus on a restricted number of locations or settings, most of which will belong to the 'standard domestic' category. Once the appropriate sets have been constructed, they can be used over and over again; and even the wear and tear sustained during the recording or filming process can contribute to the effect of reality. By the same token, clothes worn by the cast in traditional soaps tend to be items of everyday apparel. It will also be expected that once a character has appeared in a particular set of clothes, he or she will be regularly seen in that garb (partly as an aid to instant character recognition). In this way considerable savings can be made on the costume budget.

An additional, and some would claim more significant, cost-limiting factor in the making of television soaps is that the whole production process has become relatively routinized. By this one means that a group of highly trained workers are operating according to a set of working practices developed to ensure the best use of the available facilities. It is only by adhering to the strictest discipline and routine that the level of through-put can be achieved which is necessary to ensure the constant flow of programmes. The relentless pressure on a production team constantly to meet programme deadlines cannot be underestimated; and those who are professionally involved are understandably sensitive when disparaging remarks are voiced about 'assembly-line methods of production' or assumptions made that once you have served your apprenticeship in producing a soap opera you can then move on to higher things. The making of television soaps calls for exactly the same attention to detail and wide range of skills as other forms of television drama production. Some would even argue that – given the constraints under which most soap operas are produced – more skill and tenacity is needed. For whereas, in the making of series drama or putting together a single 'one-off' play, time can usually be found to re-shoot scenes or sequences, television serial producers cannot always rely on having the time to indulge in such a luxury.

Writing about soaps

By way of concluding these introductory remarks, one might add a few words about some of the problems of writing about soaps.

Because soaps have proved to be so immensely popular, they have become the subject of many studies both to explain the roots of this popularity and to reflect upon the cultural significance of such a phenomenon. They have also – and readers will need no reminding of this – become part of a major promotional industry, with a steady flow of 'coffee-table' guides and celebratory companion volumes to exploit viewers' apparently insatiable appetite for background information, pictures of star performers and nostalgic accounts of programmes' earlier days. Television soaps have likewise become the constant focus of attention in the tabloid press, with endless speculation about how story-lines will develop and with frequently titillating stories about the personal lives of actors. One of the impacts of this barrage of material has been to reinforce – or even give rise to – certain myths about how these programmes are actually produced. Any attempt at a more serious study of the soap opera phenomenon will have to address some of the more potent of these myths, with a view to presenting a more balanced and accurate picture.

The more critical analyses of the soap opera phenomenon have taken various forms. Some have attempted to come to terms with the cultural significance of soaps, whilst others have examined the question of what combination of forces makes the genre so popular. Work undertaken recently has tended to concentrate more attention on the processes by which audiences respond to, or make meanings from, soaps (see Chapter 4).

Whatever approach is adopted, however, soaps do present a particular problem to the investigator in that – unlike almost all other types of fictional text – they are by their very nature not rounded off or finished. Even when one looks back on the programmes which constitute the 'story-to-date', these often comprise hundreds, or even thousands of episodes. In other words, what one assumes to be one of the principal appeals for viewers, namely, the constantly unfolding character of the soap narrative, has always posed something of a methodological difficulty for the student of television drama serials. For in undertaking an analysis or interpretation, one is not only concerned with a retrospective survey of characters, situations and events, but is also having to weigh up the programme's potential for future development.

Because this present volume is principally designed as an introduction, the work is divided into sections which address those questions most frequently raised when soaps are discussed. The following chapter is mainly concerned with the major ingredients or characteristics of the soap genre. It looks at where and when they originated and also considers the sort of devices they most consistently employ. Chapter 3 provides an account of the various production processes involved in putting together a TV drama serial, whilst Chapter 4 gives some answers to the all-important question: 'Who watches soaps and how?'. In chapter 5 we move on to discuss one of the most vigorously debated issues in connection with soap operas: how closely they reflect the 'real' world. The final chapter broadens the discussion to consider soaps as an international phenomenon. For whilst soaps started out life fairly humbly as entertainments destined for consumption by local, and then national audiences, it was soon recognized that they had major export potential, with the result that nowadays the names of certain television soaps have acquired the sort of international reputation and status which suggests that they have succeeded in tapping into the global collective imagination.

2 What are soaps and how do they work?

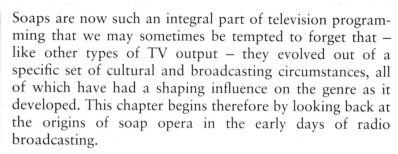

Soaps are now such an integral part of television programming that we may sometimes be tempted to forget that – like other types of TV output – they evolved out of a specific set of cultural and broadcasting circumstances, all of which have had a shaping influence on the genre as it developed. This chapter begins therefore by looking back at the origins of soap opera in the early days of radio broadcasting.

A brief history of soaps

The origins of soap opera go back to the early days of radio broadcasting in America, where detergent manufacturers and makers of other household products helped promote a form of daytime programming which would build a large and loyal audience of housewife consumers. The thinking was that, having had their attention attracted by a type of fictional material to which they could easily relate, listeners would respond more positively to the accompanying commercial messages which would spell out all the benefits to be derived from using certain consumer products. In other words, if listeners developed a trusting relationship with those responsible for the entertainment offered, they would be more likely to heed the 'suggestions' the same people had to make about what type of detergent to buy.

Mindful of the target audience, a programme format was developed which included various ingredients calculated both to appeal to an audience largely made up of women at home and to encourage regular listening habits. Predictably enough, the first American radio soaps drew quite heavily on other forms of fictional entertainment which had been shown to be popular with women. One of the most potent influences seems to have been the so-called 'domestic novel' which has a history stretching back to the middle of the eighteenth century. As the name implies, this type of literature was primarily concerned with issues centred on house and home. Women characters were always to the fore in such stories, many of which incidentally were written by women. A frequent focus of attention in these novels was on issues such as the conflict between family or domestic commitments and emotional needs or on the difficulties experienced by the non-attached woman in making her way in a male-dominated society. Additional features of the 'domestic novel' which were later to be inherited by the early broadcast soaps are firstly the recurrent tendency to subject the above-mentioned issues to a decidedly romantic and melodramatic treatment and secondly the fact that such novels frequently adopted a serialized mode of presentation (Allen, 1985, pp. 140–50; Cantor and Pingree, 1983, pp. 20–22).

Many of the early radio soaps caught on in ways which were beyond the original expectations of the advertisers and sponsors responsible for funding them. It quickly began to be recognized what potential this particular form of programming had, and some of the larger advertising agencies were not slow to open up their own radio production departments to ensure that full advantage was taken of this newly-discovered promotional vehicle. An especially attractive aspect of radio soaps from the producers' point of view was that once a successful programme formula had been found, no further major investment was needed and the programmes could be produced at comparatively low cost.

The rapid proliferation of American radio soaps in the 1930s is also linked with the fact that the system of broadcasting as it developed in the United States was one based on commercial advertising and sponsorship. The ability of soaps to command the attention of a large number of potential customers meant the production of these programmes became something of a growth industry, with rival groups vying with each other to hire the best available talent. The growth in popularity of soaps is also connected with the expansion in radio services during this period. Initially radio had confined itself to providing local services, but it was quickly recognized that much richer pickings could be made if broadcasts were made nationwide. By the early 1930s a national network system had been established, and it was thanks to this expanded system that radio serials like *Ma Perkins* and *One Man's Family* were able to reach out and capture the imagination of a huge audience. Of all the programme categories developed at the time, radio soaps proved by far the most successful in terms of both the sponsor support they generated and of their popularity with audiences. And from the point of view of the broadcasters soaps were also a desirable asset in that they were the most profitable programme category.

The proliferation of soap operas in America was not matched, however, by developments this side of the Atlantic. In Britain such a populist strand of programming was greeted by controllers at the BBC with suspicion, if not actual aversion, since it appeared to fly in the face of the 'high culture' aspirations of Public Service Broadcasting in its early days, especially as articulated by the BBC's first Director General, John Reith. Towards the end of the war, however, the first British soap *The Robinsons* (developed out of an earlier version called *Front Line Family*) did finally see the light of day. Transmitted on the Light Programme, *The Robinsons* became extremely popular, and thus paved the way for the post-war 'classic' BBC radio soaps *Mrs Dale's Diary* (1948–1969) and *The Archers*, the longest-running radio serial ever produced, which started life in 1950. In spite of the fact that *Mrs Dale's Diary* and *The Archers* were to become something approaching national institutions, there has over the years been something less than a thorough-going commitment on the part of the BBC to the soap opera genre (whether on radio or television). This clearly shows how the 'encouragement' of certain programme formats is closely allied to the type of broadcasting system which particular nations have developed.

As to the reasons why this form of programming came to be known as 'soap opera', whilst it is not chronicled exactly who coined the term, it probably originated in the American trade press in the late 1930s or early 1940s. The term usefully merges two of the components which had been most closely associated with the development of the genre up to that point. 'Soap' alludes to the role played by the large detergent manufacturers (especially Procter and Gamble) in exploiting daytime serials as a vehicle for advertising and promotion. 'Opera' is taken to be a reference to the fact that most soap dramas had a marked tendency to be rather larger than life and often prone to indulge in melodramatic excess. There is of course a certain irony in suggesting that soaps are 'operatic' in that one of the claims made about the genre is that it attempts to capture something of the ordinariness of everyday life!

Television takes over
Soaps have – in that time-honoured phrase – come a long way since those early radio days, when listeners were introduced to the latest developments in the story by a friendly narrator-guide who also acted as the sponsor's representative extolling the virtues of a particular cleaning agent. The most obvious change is that radio serials have largely been supplanted by TV soaps, to the extent that the former might even be regarded as something of an endangered species. In the United States in the immediate post-war period there was a steep decline in the number of daytime radio serials being produced for and by the networks, and by the mid-1950s critics were able to declare that the 'radio era of the soap opera' was over (Cantor and Pingree, 1983, p. 39). Within a commercially driven broadcasting system sponsors and advertisers rightly saw that television now afforded them much better prospects of reaching a mass

audience and thus they began to commit energies and resources to the development of television soaps.

Though many of those working in the broadcasting industry were persuaded of the long-term potential of television, there was initial uncertainty as how best to manage the transition from one medium to the other. Radio serials had become so immensely popular with audiences that there were some fears as to whether this successful formula could actually be made to work in a different medium. One anxiety was that television engaged both the visual and aural attention of the audience, so that housewives might actually be diverted from carrying out the household chores at the same time as keeping abreast of the story. Since the major objective of soap opera producers in the United States remained that of securing the attention of ever larger numbers of women at home in order to persuade them to buy a range of named consumer products, television was regarded by the more sceptical advertisers as being of less importance than some might have predicted. An additional fear on the part of producers was that the production costs for television were much greater than those of radio, so the risk factor would be correspondingly higher.

Once the television bandwagon began to roll, however, most of these misgivings quickly evaporated. It was soon realized that in the longer term television would be the medium which would attract the mass audience. The post-war development of the soap opera therefore is one that sees the gradual displacement of radio soaps by their television counterparts. One noteworthy feature of this television take-over is that, in spite of those initial fears, the soap opera formula appeared to work just as well in the new medium. In the United States this meant that one or two of the most successful radio soaps could simply be converted into the more popular format and carry the audience with them. One of the best known American soaps *The Guiding Light*, for instance, began as a radio programme in 1937, then for a period (1952–1956) went out in 'parallel' television and radio versions, before continuing life in a television-only format.

In general a clear line of development can be drawn between the early radio soaps – particularly as they evolved in the 1930s and 1940s in the United States – and their post-war TV equivalents. For one thing, many of the writers and producers who had made a name for themselves in conceiving or producing radio serials were hired to work on television soaps. Also the companies and organizations responsible for generating the programmes had for the most part gained their initial broadcasting experience in radio. This meant that many of the television soaps carried some of the same institutional marks as their radio forbears. (The National Broadcasting Company [NBC] and the Columbia Broadcasting System [CBS] were the two major players in this respect.) Additional features which these early television soaps have in common with the daytime radio serials was that they were transmitted daily (5 episodes a week); that they were targeted at a largely female audience; and that most of them went out live (with all the attendant hazards that live transmission entailed). Given all these affinities, some critics indeed began to wonder whether it would not be more appropriate to use the phrase 'radio with pictures' to describe the phenomenon of television soap, at least as far as the daytime programmes were concerned.

The long-running American soap *The Guiding Light* (**Procter and Gamble Productions, Incorporated**)

Daytime and prime-time soaps

As television soaps began to feature ever more prominently in the daytime schedules of the American networks, thought was also given as to whether soap operas might be successfully introduced into the prime-time, evening schedules. The only misgivings, how-ever, were that the slow-moving narratives of the daytime soaps might not be sufficiently arresting to appeal to a mixed audience which was looking for a more action-filled type of entertainment. The assumption was that to capture and retain the attention of prime-time viewers it would be necessary to devise a form of drama which had some of the spectacular and gripping qualities often associated with the Hollywood film. In some ways therefore the requirements of prime-time programming ran counter to much of what the traditional soap opera had to offer. In the words of one critic, prime-time programmes 'depend upon unrelenting action and conflict, having little time for the development of subtlety and nuance, thus placing the viewer in the position of being an onlooker rather than an active participant' (Cassata and Skill, 1983, pp. xv-xvi). Predictably enough, what happened was that a 'hybrid' form of prime-time dramatic entertainment emerged which combined some of the design features of traditional soaps with techniques and strategies employed in Hollywood-style film production. Considerably more money has been invested in producing these prime-time soaps and there has been a general attempt to extend what were evidently considered to be the limited horizons of the daytime serial. The viewer is, for instance, often carried beyond the narrowly defined bounds of a single, community-based setting. Indeed, as the competition for audiences has become more intense, it seemed as if a rivalry developed as to who could dream up still more exotic locations for the sequence of melodramatic events designed to keep the viewers enthralled.

Peyton Place (ABC Television)

Ed Nelson and Dorothy Malone, stars of *Peyton Place*

There has, understandably, been a good deal of debate about whether these prime-time productions deserve to be included in the soap opera category. In some respects prime-time serials like *Peyton Place* (1964–1969) and the hugely successful *Dallas* have been seen to have as much in common with television series drama as they do with the somewhat more everyday world of soaps. Individual episodes go out once or twice weekly, in contrast to the daily transmission of traditional soaps. There is also a tendency for these prime-time serials to be presented in blocks of episodes which comprise a season's viewing. The break between these seasons has the effect of detracting somewhat from the illusion that one is caught up in an uninterrupted flow of events (one of the main hallmarks of the traditional soap). Individual episodes of prime-time serials also have a higher degree of self-containment, in other words, there is not the same sense of continuousness that is achieved by daytime serials.

Whilst there are significant differences between the more glossy, faster-moving prime-time serials and their daytime equivalents, they have sufficient in common for us to consider them both in this type of introductory study. The fact that most viewers also regard the likes of *Dallas* and *Dynasty* as belonging to the soap genre is a further reason for not excluding them from our considerations. In order to point up their distinctive characteristic, however, we shall refer to them henceforth as 'supersoaps'.

Meanwhile in Britain . . .

Though many of the prime-time American serials have been eagerly lapped up by television audiences in Britain, soaps in this country have developed along rather different lines to their American counterparts. By and large, British soaps have more in common with American daytime soaps than they do with the prime-time variety and appear for this reason to be more down-to-earth. As in the United States, it has been the commercial broadcasting system which has been most closely associated with the production and screening of soaps, even though the BBC has scored some notable individual successes in its time.

Possibly encouraged by the success of *Mrs Dale's Diary* and *The Archers*, it was in fact the BBC who in 1954 launched the first British TV soap *The Grove Family*, which built a large and loyal following before its rather premature demise in 1957. After the arrival of commercial television in 1955, however, a new impetus was given to the genre, and several of the ITV companies were soon making a bid to develop a soap which would pull in a mass audience. ATV's *Emergency Ward Ten* which went on the air in

An early British soap: *The Grove Family* (BBC Television)

Emergency Ward Ten (ATV), one of the early medical soaps

1957 gave an early indication of how popular medical soaps could be with audiences, but it was Granada Television who really struck gold when in December 1960 they broadcast the opening episode of *Coronation Street*. *The Street*, as it is popularly known, has proved to be the longest-running serial on British television. The only other soap which came anywhere near *The Street* in terms of ratings in these early years was *Crossroads*. This programme, which was started by ATV in 1964, had an altogether more chequered history, however. Although it was very popular with viewers, it was constantly derided by the critics. Nevertheless it displayed considerable staying power, until it was finally terminated – after many trials and tribulations – in 1988.

Seeing just how popular some of the ITV soaps were, the BBC rose to the challenge and produced in the course of the 1960s two or three soaps of its own. *Compact* (1962–5) was a bi-weekly serial set in the offices of a women's magazine. *United* (1965–7), another bi-weekly, followed the ups and downs of a football team, whilst *The*

Newcomers (1965–9) followed the fortunes of several London families settling in a new rural environment. None of these soaps, however, caught on in the same way as the more popular ITV soaps and – in spite of various further ventures into continuous serial drama in the intervening years – the BBC did not produce any ratings-topping soap until the arrival of *EastEnders* in 1985.

The ITV companies meanwhile – spurred on by the continuing success of *Coronation Street* and *Crossroads* – developed ever more variations on the soap opera theme. Imported American soaps (including the then notorious *Peyton Place*) began to appear in the ITV schedules. Regional soaps, that is those produced by the regionally based ITV companies, also began to make their mark. Some programmes, like Harlech Television's *Taff Acre* (1981), a rural soap set in South Wales, were relatively short-lived. Others, including Yorkshire Television's *Emmerdale* (1972–) and Scottish Television's *Take the High Road* (1980–) proved to be far more popular, not just in the region from which they emanated, but also, as time went by, throughout the ITV network. At least part of the success of both these programmes is attributable to the beauty of the rural surroundings in which the action is set, which affords an agreeable contrast to the urban setting of *The Street* and later of *EastEnders*.

A soap with a chequered history: *Crossroads* (ATV/Central)

The Newcomers (BBC Television)

Even an introductory survey of the development of British soaps would not be complete without a brief mention of *Brookside*. The programme, now a tri-weekly serial, was launched in November 1982, to coincide with the beginning of Channel 4, part of whose remit was a particular commitment to innovative programming. Whilst soap opera in itself hardly constitutes an innovative format, *Brookside* set itself the task of using the vehicle of television serial drama to explore a range of social issues in frank and often challenging ways. *Brookside* has for this reason not always had an easy relationship with the 'moral watchdogs' who have regularly discovered examples of left-wing propaganda in the programme; but for many critics it represents an important advance in terms of what television soaps can aspire to.

With the ever increasing number of television channels and the move towards a progressively deregulated system, it is likely that in the coming years soap opera will continue to play an important role in TV programme schedules. Satellite broadcasters are already providing an outlet for various forms of soap entertainment, much of it originating from Australia or the United States. At the same time, companies are constantly experimenting with ideas for new drama serials, many of which founder, however, at the drawing-board stage. One idea that has recently got off the ground before the company itself foundered was a British Satellite Broadasting (BSB) programme called *Jupiter Moon*, which was set in the ultimate exotic location of an orbiting space station.

Having briefly surveyed some of the major landmarks in the history of soap opera's development, we now move on to consider the question of what are the most characteristic features of the genre.

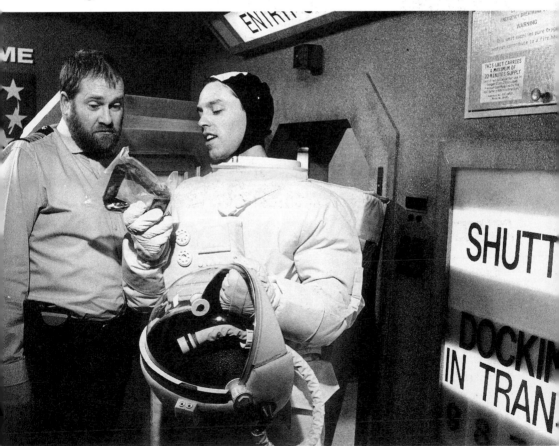

The first extra-terrestrial soap: *Jupiter Moon* **(shown on BSB)**

What is soap opera?

A never-ending story

> Author (to teenage viewer in central Scotland – November 1989):
> 'Could you please define what you think television soaps are?'
> Viewer: 'Well – it's things like *Coronation Street* or *Neighbours* . . .
> You know, never-ending stories!'

This is quite a typical response when people are asked for a definition of television soaps. The naming of two well-known TV drama serials shows first of all that viewers are in no doubt as to what category of programme is covered by the term 'soap'. It also underlines, however, the degree to which people's idea of 'soap watching' has become tied to particular examples of the soap genre. In other words, as a viewer you may very well have a considerable, though unarticulated, fund of knowledge as to what soaps are and how they work, but your major concern is always with the individual model rather than with more abstract questions of design. (An appropriate analogy might be that of driving a car. Most drivers are more concerned with the performance which the car delivers – whether measured in terms of comfort, speed or reliability – than with the details of engine configuration, gear ratio and the like.)

The one element picked out in our teenage viewer's definition which does constitute a design characteristic, however, is that they are 'never-ending stories'. The fact that soaps consist of unfolding narratives where individual story-lines are carried over from one episode to the next is the feature which most clearly separates them from other forms of broadcast drama. Whereas other types of narrative fiction are working their way towards some suitable or satisfactory ending (whether after one or a series of episodes), for soaps there can be no such act of closure. No clearly defined moment of resolution can ever be attained. They are forever projecting us – and the lives of their fictional characters – into the future, always persuading us that there are sufficient delights and surprises in store to make it worth our while to continue watching.

The characteristic openness of soaps does not, however, mean that they are completely devoid of endings. The most radical ending of course, is when, for whatever reason, the whole programme is given a death sentence and reasonably plausible ways have to be sought to close down, or at least put into a kind of limbo, the major story-lines. In those cases where the soap in question has had quite a short, and possibly unhappy, life, this 'killing-off' process can be effected without creating a major stir. But where a serial is terminated after having run for many years with a large and loyal follow-

***Dallas* (Lorimar Television)**

ing, the decision to end it almost always leads to various displays of resentment on the part of the audience, who in one sense have invested a part of their emotional selves in the world which that particular soap evokes.

Even though soap narratives are constantly casting an eye to the future, there are no small number of instances where endings of a kind do occur. Characters, some of whom possibly have been with the serial for many years, are for a variety of reasons written out of the script (see p. 66–7). Story-lines, some of which may also have been developed over a considerable period of time, may be 'reined in' as certain situations reach the stage where they can be plausibly

resolved. Conflicts between characters on which the narrative may
have fed for many a long month (soaps thrive on ongoing sagas) can
be temporarily resolved by one of the standard fictional ploys by
which either a reconciliation or a clean break is brought about.
What is important about these moments of temporary resolution is
that they should never be allowed to become an end in themselves.
This is why those occasions where a degree of harmony has clearly
been achieved (e.g. a wedding celebration) are frequently made to
serve as the seedbed for future conflicts.

The unfolding text

Another feature of traditional soaps that is often remarked upon is
their slow narrative progression. The emphasis in the world of the
traditional soap is not on a rapid succession of dramatic events but
on a set of characters living out their lives in an environment which
may not be all that different from that of the viewer. What further
reinforces the feeling that one is witnessing scenes of 'everyday life'
is the fact that the majority of issues or problems broached in the
course of the narrative have to do with personal or domestic
matters, especially those relating to family or group relationships.
The sense of realism is especially enhanced, however, by the relatively slow pace at which the story is allowed to proceed. It is as if
events were unfolding in real time. The illusion is created that events
in the world of the soap are evolving or running in parallel with
those in the sphere of reality. Whereas other types of narrative are
often characterized by a strong sense of relentless forward movement towards inevitable climax or resolution, soaps are wholly
lacking in such compulsion[1]. The result is that for most viewers
soaps seem to be more closely aligned with their own experience of
time unfolding, a fact which may partly explain why so many in the
audience are disposed to believe in the 'reality' of soaps. One further
consequence of this slow narrative progression is that the illusion is
also created that soap characters are leading what one critic has
referred to as an 'unrecorded existence' in the days and hours
between the individual episodes (Dyer *et al.* 1981, p. 10).

---

1   Some critics have for this reason considered soaps to be a
particularly 'feminine' type of narrative. Because soaps are by
definition open-ended texts, it is maintained that they offer a
refreshing contrast to the more 'masculine' text where the
primary impulse is always towards resolution and closure.
For more on this idea see Tania Modleski 'The Search for
Tomorrow in Today's Soap Operas' in *Loving with a
Vengeance: Mass-produced Fantasies for Women*, 1982, pp.
85–109.

Dallas – **Bobby versus JR**

It is in relation to the 'slowly unfolding text' that the greatest contrasts emerge between the traditional or daytime serials and the altogether brasher supersoaps. Whereas the former will probably take several episodes to build towards a climatic moment, the likes of *Dallas* or *Dynasty* will aim to include several such moments in each episode. One can also be fairly certain that the full dramatic potential will be extracted from these exchanges or confrontations. Traditional soaps operate according to a different set of principles. Here the emphasis is on chronicling the build-up and aftermath of a significant or dramatic event rather than concentrating on the spectacular impact of the event itself. A good illustration of this point was provided in a recent episode of *Brookside*. A teenage couple, Sammy (Samantha) and Owen accept a lift from a couple of young men in a stolen car and are involved in a serious crash in which there are two fatalities. The crash sequence itself is filmed using some of the conventions of the crime thriller and in this respect generates considerable suspense. The main narrative importance of the incident, however, lies not so much in the drama of the chase as what it makes possible in subsequent episodes: the scenes in hospital as Sammy visits Owen lying in a coma, the police inquiries into the incident, the discussion amongst family and friends about how it all happened and last but not least some general reflections on the whole issue of joyriding.

Cliff-hangers and tease devices

In the case of the *Brookside* incident described above, the crash itself occurred – predictably enough – at the very end of an episode, with no indication of how many, if any, of the car's occupants had survived. This is one of those time-honoured 'cliff-hangers' where the audience is left in considerable suspense about what the next episode will reveal. Cliff-hangers are usually considered to be a standard feature of most kinds of serial drama, of whatever format. The calculation on the part of the producers is that if sheer force of habit is not sufficient to get you to watch the next episode, then the curiosity to know 'what happens next' will. Cliff-hangers of the high-tension, car crash variety are, however, comparatively rare in traditional soaps, though there is some evidence to suggest that their frequency count increases, if the soap in question has been going through a poor patch as far as audience ratings are concerned.

The more usual strategies for taking temporary leave of an audience at the end of an episode are ones involving a more muted type of 'cliff-hanger'. Viewers are not so much left on tenterhooks as manoeuvred into a position where they find themselves playing through what implications the latest twist in the narrative has for the life of the community or for the relationship between individual characters. Typical of these 'leave-taking' devices are situations in which a character receives an unexpected piece of news or suddenly discovers something which had, for whatever reason, previously been withheld from them, though not always from the audience. Such moments of revelation or discovery have in fact become such a standard convention in television serials that they are now one of the most frequently parodied items of the soap opera format. In many cases the imminent arrival of these moments is signalled by having the camera close in on the face of the character concerned in order that the audience can more readily identify with what the person is going through. At the same time, because these final reaction shots are rarely accompanied by any utterance on the character's part, they are ideal vehicles for encouraging speculation about the future course of the narrative (see also p. 100).

One of the particular pleasures of soap-watching, according to many viewers, is closely connected with the various expectations elicited by these cliff-hanger or teasing devices. Teasing occurs when it hangs in the balance whether certain expectations will be fulfilled in quite the manner one has anticipated; or when one is conscious that the other party, in this case the script-writing team, is in some way playing with these same expectations. There is, in other words, a clear recognition on the part of the audience that in becoming a follower of a particular soap, one is involving oneself in an elaborate guessing-game. One of the unwritten contracts of those who write soap operas therefore is that they will always produce an adequate number of narrative clues to allow audiences to follow events as they unfold, but at the same time will keep viewers on their toes by encouraging speculation and occasionally laying false trails.

Dallas spinoff – *Knott's Landing*

Interweaving storylines

Leaving an audience at the end of each episode in some uncertainty as to what course the future narrative will take is an effective strategy for bridging the barren period between episodes. Other techniques are used, however, for maintaining interest and exciting expectation within each episode. Chief among these is the device of segmenting the narrative in such a way that one is constantly being switched between three or four separate story-lines. The constant switching between story-lines can involve as many as thirty or more scene-switches in the course of a thirty-minute soap episode, though this interweaving has become such an accepted part of the grammar of soaps that the overall impression is one of seamless flow. There is of course a common element in the story-lines in that they are all woven around the lives of a set number of characters who constitute the soap's 'dramatis personae'.

Amnesia is the problem for Val in _Knott's Landing_

One of the additional effects of this intertwining is to provide a measure of narrative variety, which in turn allows viewers to be kept in touch with the lives of a relatively large number of characters. Moving back and forth between a number of different domestic and social spaces also has the effect of contributing to the 'realism' of the fiction, as it reinforces the illusion that we are mobile observers privileged to witness events from more than a single perspective.

The interweaving of story-lines also enables certain other effects to be created which are typical of the soap genre. For instance, it encourages viewers to make connections between characters and events in these separate narrative strands. One might have one strand in which a character is bitterly complaining about the difficulty of making ends meet, whilst simultaneously, in stark contrast, in another story-line two characters may be congratulating each other on their good fortune in pulling off a major business coup. A more subtle form of interweaving occurs in those situations where, to the uninitiated viewer, there is no apparent relationship between events in the separate story-lines. Viewers of several years' standing, however, may very well be able to call on their store of accumulated knowledge to make quite significant connections. Take a situation, let us say, where in one story-line a mother is having a heated argument with a renegade daughter, whilst in the story-line with which it alternates a young wife is involved in a serious matrimonial dispute with her spouse. In the course of the mother/daughter argument various accusations are made which remind the viewer of earlier difficulties encountered by the young wife with her parents many years previously – and which may have a bearing on her present dilemma. In this way the interweaving of story-lines can be a device for opening up the viewers' memory bank, thus creating resonances which would be difficult to achieve in other fictional forms.

A central core of characters

The interweaving of separate story-lines has come to be accepted as one of the major structuring principles of soaps; even though on exceptional occasions it has been known for one story-line to 'carry' a whole episode. The constant switching between scenes can only really work, however, if the viewers are already familiar with the characters who occupy the story-lines. Viewer familiarity with the central core of a serial's characters lies at the heart of the soap opera experience. As we have already had occasion to comment, viewers can develop a deep attachment to these fictional figures who may come to play as prominent a part in their lives as close relatives.

Most soaps operate with a complement of twenty characters or more, not all of whom will necessarily be deployed at the same time. The number of 'regular' characters in soaps is almost always higher than that in series. This is to ensure that sufficient characters are available to be mobilized in the main story-lines which are running at any one time. In addition to this central core of characters around which most of the narrative revolves, various new characters are imported from time to time. In some cases the newcomers are necessary in order to introduce a twist in the narrative or even a major plot development. Sometimes, as happened recently in the case of the Scottish soap *Take the High Road*, several new characters may make their entrance at the same time as part of a general refurbishment exercise. As with other forms of dramatic fiction, the introduction of incomers can often be used as a device for creating discord or trouble in the community or neighbourhood they enter. They may challenge the established values or even display decidedly villainous traits. When the latter occurs, the incomers will almost inevitably receive their come-uppance at the hands of community representatives and frequently will be drummed out of town or neighbourhood. Alternatively, having learned their lesson and indicated they are willing to conform, they may be absorbed into the central core of major players.

A central core of characters: the lead players in Scottish Television's *Take the High Road*

The task of assembling a core of characters who will plausibly fit the chosen setting for the soap and to whom an audience will be able to relate is one of the most crucial aspects in the planning of any soap. In some individual cases one is fortunate in having quite a detailed chronicle of the processes involved in conceiving and developing an idea for a new soap. The originators of the BBC soap *EastEnders* provide one such account, which among other things, allows one to gauge the principal criteria by which the central core of characters was chosen. Thus, according to the initial blueprint for the show, the serial would focus on 'the life of a community in the East End of London' and there would be 'a healthy mix of multi-racial, larger-than-life characters' (Smith and Holland, 1987, p. 19). Characters would display a range of 'Cockney' attributes, in particular the capacity to be 'lively, tough, proud and sharply funny'. They would also have a strong sense of belonging to a clearly defined, traditional community. The setting in which most of the action would take place would be a 'fairly run-down Victorian square' to which most of the inhabitants would feel a fierce territorial allegiance.

The other major blueprint-specification relating to the central core of *EastEnders* characters was that they should be members of individual family groups or households. Witnessing a group of characters interacting in a domestic environment is virtually a generic requirement of soaps, but the chosen East End setting would make it that much easier to devise plausible platforms for dramatic interaction, since 'families and family life play a large part in East End culture: families are frequently large, matriarchal and often with several generations living under the same roof'. As a further aid to facilitate character interaction, *EastEnders* – again in common with the majority of other soaps – would have a series of meeting-places ('a pub, a mini-supermarket, a launderette, a caff, and . . . a lively street market') in order to provide the opportunity for those chance encounters which play such an important role in the majority of soap narratives.

Decisions concerning what particular individuals to introduce into the regular cast of characters will also rest on a number of factors. First there is the question of credibility: whether one could plausibly meet such types in the chosen setting. To meet this criterion, producers will normally attempt to introduce a reasonable cross-section of figures who represent different aspects of 'life in the community'. Introducing a broad mix of characters also increases the possibility that individual members of the audience will be able to identify with at least one of the central core. And from the production team's point of view, having access to a comparatively large number of characters makes the task of generating interesting new story-lines slightly less daunting than it might have been. As the producers of *EastEnders* observed as they were working on their blueprint: 'The larger the mix of people the easier it will be to find stories that have variety, interest and mileage' (ibid; p. 57).

A women's genre?

One feature of soaps that has been often commented on over the years is that female characters play a more positive role than in many other types of dramatic fiction. This characteristic – which some critics consider to be a defining or generic feature of soaps – is clearly linked with the fact that drama serials, at least in their first few decades, were mainly targeted at an audience of women. Producing a range of female characters to whom the audience could easily relate, or with whom they could positively identify, was one of the strategies by which ratings could be maintained and advertisers or sponsors kept happy.

Matriarchal figures: Miss Ellie in *Dallas*

It is not just the abundance and range of female characters which is striking in soaps, it is also the type of roles in which they appear. In contrast to more traditional, stereotypical depictions of women which frequently reduce them to the level of passive sex objects, female characters in soaps are often figures of great strength and resourcefulness. This is not to suggest that the majority of women in soaps fall into this category, but in most serials there will normally be one or two who, by force of personality or by their independent spirit, command the respect – if not awe – of those around them. Matriarchal figures such as Miss Ellie in *Dallas* or Lou Beale in *EastEnders* are encountered with relative frequency. In the world of soap opera where strife and stress of many kinds abound, the matriarch can display rock-like or 'sheet anchor' qualities of stability. As archetypal 'copers' or in their 'wise woman' capacity as heads of a dynasty, they also represent the final court of appeal when it comes to sorting out conflict or dissent in the family ranks.

Another strong woman: Ena Sharples from *Coronation Street*

In stark contrast to the matriarch, there is another category of female character in soaps. Here the woman's role is conceived less in terms of keeping family and home intact than remaining a free and independent spirit. The drive to remain independent may take several forms. There is, for instance, the strong-willed ruthless woman who will stop at nothing to achieve her goals and will even gain satisfaction from the discomfiture of any rivals (male or female) who get in her way. This type is often to the fore in the American supersoaps and is possibly best epitomized by the go-getting, man-eating Alexis Rowan (played by Joan Collins) in *Dynasty*. Many of the British soaps on the other hand are marked by the presence of women – most of them no longer in the prime of youth – who have remained sturdily independent, in spite of sometimes quite strong social or family pressures to be otherwise. As such their judgement is respected and they often operate as confidantes or advisors to the young, vulnerable or inexperienced. Bet Lynch and Rita Fairclough in *Coronation Street* are good examples of this particular type of strong woman.

   To the extent that strong female characters have often been to the fore in soaps and attention has been mostly concentrated on the family and domestic domain, male characters have tended not to enjoy the same prominence as in more action-orientated genres. Men have by and large been cast in quite stereotypical roles: as joke-cracking pub landlord, irascible family father, eligible bachelor and the like. As attitudes in society have changed, however, soaps have reflected something of this change by introducing a number of male characters who are altogether more complex or sensitive personalities and can no longer be equated with the former stereotypes. Of the British soaps currently being broadcast *Brookside* – which in some ways set out to break the mould of the traditional serial – is the one which has most clearly challenged the view that soaps are essentially 'women's fiction'. The day when an all-male soap will be broadcast is, however, probably still some way off!

Dynasty: the fight in the swimming pool

3 How are television soaps produced?

In this chapter we shall be exploring a number of issues relating to the making of television soaps, principally the *contexts* in which the production takes place and the main *processes* involved in the putting together of a TV drama serial. Restrictions of space mean that we will only be able to cover the broader aspects of production, although, where appropriate, readers will be directed to accounts which give a far more detailed description of how individual soap operas reach our screens.

A further objective of the chapter will be to correct certain popular, but mistaken, notions of how soaps are actually produced. This is not to suggest that many viewers are of the belief that soap actors and actresses are making it up as they go along, but there is a distinct danger – particularly given the style of reporting in some of the tabloid journals – that some phases or aspects of production will be given a much higher profile than others. The constant stream of tabloid stories about the lives and loves of leading players in soaps may, for instance, give a very exaggerated impression of their importance within the larger production cycle and obscure the role of others in the production hierarchy. A more accurate idea of how soaps are made is provided by the occasional behind-the-scenes television documentaries and the chapters in those 'official companion' volumes which address production issues. Here again the picture that readers or viewers get may well be somewhat partial, since the works in question are generally conceived as part of a promotional drive to sustain interest in the soap in question, so any major problems which have been encountered in, say, financing the serial, tend not to be given particular prominence.

Who produces what?

A somewhat different approach to the issue of production is to start by asking questions about what is actually being produced. The common-sense response to such an enquiry is that the combined evidence of tens of thousands of TV soap episodes all emanating from the same source should leave one in little doubt as to who is producing what. Adopting only a slightly different perspective, however, it is just as feasible to conclude that the audience itself is crucially involved in the business of production. Viewers are not so much passive recipients of what television offers, but rather are active participants in the production process – in the sense that they do not simply read off the meanings implanted there by a producer-author but produce their own meanings through a more active process, which can be thought of as one of negotiation.[1] The claim that meanings are generated principally in the minds of viewers or readers is one which can be applied to a wide variety of both literary and visual texts, but it seems especially applicable in the case of soap opera. As we shall discover in the following chapter, soaps encourage a very active form of response from audiences. It is out of this constant exchange of views and speculation that the 'meanings' of soap opera are produced. As Taylor and Mullan observe in their discussion of audience viewing habits, largely based on a study of soaps: 'it seems that television drama has only properly occurred, been thoroughly realised, when the plots and the moral messages they contain have been discussed and interpreted and re-dramatised in the company of friends or mere acquaintances' (1987, p. 206).

As well as asking questions about *how* meanings are produced, one can also legitimately begin to ask questions about *what* is being produced in soap opera. Again the obvious response is to observe that the evidence, say in the form of 30 years of *Coronation Street*, is plainly there for all to see. An alternative view, however, is to say that it is not a regular supply of television entertainment that is being produced, but a large and loyal contingent of viewers. As one critic of the soap genre put it most succinctly: 'One does not have to be a cynic to hold the view that television transforms viewers into units of economic exchange' (Allen, 1985, p. 45). Since one of the highest priorities of commercial television has been to deliver viewers into the hands of advertisers (TV advertising rates are measured in terms of what it costs to 'reach' a thousand viewers), it is not difficult to see why such reliable audience-producing programmes as soaps should always have featured prominently in commercial schedules.[2]

---

1   For more on this idea of the 'active reader' see in particular the work of Roland Barthes, especially his essay 'The Death of the Author' in *Image-Music-Text*, 1977, pp. 142–148.

2   One has only to look at the daytime schedules of American television to see the extent to which soap operas are indeed 'commodifying' the television audience. In one survey – conducted in the early 1980s by *Newsweek* – it was calculated that the 13 regular daytime soaps put out each weekday by the ABC, CBS and NBC networks were responsible for bringing in well over 15% of the networks' total advertising revenue (Flitterman, 1983, p. 85).

Whilst it may be appropriate to talk of audiences being produced for advertisers within a television system largely financed out of advertising, how is one to understand the economics of soap opera production within the non-commercial sphere? As we have already had occasion to comment, over the years the BBC has had something less than a thorough-going commitment to soap opera production, believing that pandering too much to popular taste might undermine its other important aim of providing a measure of cultural enlightenment. On the other hand the corporation has at times turned to the continuous drama serial (preferred BBC terminology) when it felt it needed to compete with ITV for the television audience. Many observers, for instance, have seen the arrival of *EastEnders* in the mid-1980s as directly resulting from the BBC's urgent need to produce a big ratings success at a time when the corporation was being made to feel that it was vulnerable to various forms of attack (Buckingham, 1987, pp. 117–8).

The high ratings obtained by *EastEnders* have therefore, in the opinion of many observers, proved a valuable asset in the corporation's continuing quest to obtain adequate levels of funding through the government-supervised licence fee system. The programme has also proved to have economic potential in its own right. It has sold well abroad (see pp. 106–7) and has also provided the BBC with many opportunities for commercial exploitation. This can take the form of direct spin-offs from the programme itself (home-videos, books based on the lives of earlier generations of 'East Enders') or can be one of various types of merchandising (sales of T-shirts, mugs and other desirable commodities).

Taking the lid off TV soap production

Various factors have to be taken into account when talking about the production of TV soaps. One major consideration is that they are made for the most part by or for large broadcasting institutions or companies and will, for this reason, be subject to a whole series of institutional constraints and influences. These range from what funds are initially made available to start a project, to what niche it is envisaged the programme will occupy in a particular broadcasting schedule, or what production resources – in the form of studio and technical facilities – can be allocated on a fairly long-term basis. All this means that whilst at any one time creative minds are spawning many new ideas or scenarios for new soaps, only a small proportion of them stand a chance of ever getting beyond the 'initial outline' stage. As to who determines what programmes actually go into production, this decision usually lies with a small group of individuals at the head of some organizational hierarchy, whether this be the management staff of Procter and Gamble Productions Inc. or top executives at the BBC.

Whilst it is not always possible to account for all the forces – institutional and otherwise – which have affected the production of a particular soap opera, one cannot underestimate the importance of budgetary matters. The glossiness of the American soaps, especially supersoaps like *Dallas* and *Dynasty*, has much to do with the generous budgets which are made available (though the phenomenal international success of these products more than justifies the high production costs). On the other hand, where production teams are working within much tighter budgets, modes of production will have to be employed which will balance the demand for a quality product with the financial limitations under which they are operating. In Europe, for instance, we are now seeing a growing number of examples of soap operas made by much smaller production teams on relatively low budgets.[3]

Though budgets have an important determining influence on the sort of soaps that are produced, there are also other factors which have to be taken into account. Developments in the structures of broadcasting can in themselves often lead to changes in techniques or modes of production. In Britain, for instance, we have witnessed over the last few years a significant increase in the number of small or medium-sized television companies, as demand for out-of-house programme making has grown (partly as a result of the arrival of Channel 4 and partly as a consequence of government encouragement of the independent production sector). These companies have not only been responsible for various types of new-look programming, they have also on occasions devised certain innovatory production techniques. The company which makes the Channel 4 soap *Brookside*, Phil Redmond's Liverpool-based Mersey Television, is a good example of the successful introduction of new – and Redmond would argue more effective – procedures for putting together a tri-weekly serial.

In the case of *Brookside* this has involved acquiring a number of houses on a small private estate and fitting them out in such a way that they could form a permanent set. This has not only brought

3   In 1984 Swiss German-language television (DRS) in Zurich started broadcasting a weekly TV drama serial *Motel* (was it inspired by *Crossroads*?) which was put together by a small production team working within the constraints of a very tight budget and operating with late production deadlines (Bichsel, 1984, pp. 13–15).

Dynasty: terrorists attack on the royal wedding of Amanda Carrington to Prince Michael. Blake and Krystle find their lives under threat

benefits in the shape of reduced costs, it also has enabled recording to take place in a situation far removed from the 'artificiality' of the large studio-based television factories; the claim being that one is better able to capture a live atmosphere in this way and thus convey a greater sense of realism.

Cost advantages of soaps
The examples cited above give some indication of the different modes which can be employed in the production of TV drama serials. At one end of the scale there are the American supersoaps which are for the most part not only recorded on film but use many of the techniques we associate with Hollywood-style film making. At the other end of the scale we have relatively modest, small-scale productions where the emphasis is on cost efficiency and quite a short production cycle. In the following section we shall confine ourselves mainly to looking at what goes into the production of the more traditional type of bi-or tri-weekly soap, such as *EastEnders*

or *Coronation Street*, since these are the programmes with which readers will probably be most familiar.

From the point of view of broadcasters, soaps always have the advantage of being much less costly than other forms of TV drama, especially if the very large audiences which a soap can usually be relied on to generate are included in the calculations. The reasons for soaps' relative cost-effectiveness are not difficult to fathom. Whereas in the case of series drama each new self-contained episode will normally require substantial investment in new sets or costumes, soaps – with their restricted number of recurring settings and their traditional emphasis on the everyday world of domestic interiors – make far fewer material demands. Soaps are in this respect extremely economical, even though there has been something of a tendency in recent years to include a larger number of scenes shot on location which can in some circumstances cause a substantial increase to the overall cost.

The initial start-up costs for a programme can of course involve substantial investment, so with all new soap projects much time and thought is devoted to 'product development'. With American soaps

The settings for the Channel 4 soap *Brookside* and BBC's *Eastenders*

this will often entail the pre-testing of the product on selected groups of viewers and then introducing whatever changes are thought necessary in the light of subsequent comments. In addition, with all new ventures into soap opera the most careful consideration is given to how the new product can be made sufficiently distinctive and attractive to compete with long-established programmes on rival channels, while retaining many or all of those features which audiences expect to find in standard soap entertainment.

Once a new soap has been successfully launched, however, the benefits from the broadcasters' point of view may well be incremental. In other words, the longer a particular soap runs, the more

Scenes shot on location: *Brookside* **visits Rome**

economical it can appear to be. In contrast to other types of programme production, an established soap opera is an item which can be easily and regularly accounted for. In these cost-conscious times the knowledge that expensive equipment and studio resources are being utilized on this regular and intensive basis can represent a powerful economic argument to those who decide what programmes are produced. An additional factor which helps keep down the cost of soap opera production is that the salaries paid can be lower than for other types of television production. Actors appearing in traditional soaps, even though they may become household names, are only paid a fraction of the amount which the prima donnas of the supersoaps demand and receive. Other members of the production team, directors, producers and writers, have also been known to voice their dissatisfaction on occasions that the level of remuneration they receive does not always reflect the range of skills they are called on to deploy.

One should perhaps hasten to add, however, that complaints about soaps being under-resourced are heard less frequently nowadays than they once were. Yet there was a time not so long ago when soaps were viewed as being virtually beyond the pale in terms of production standards. Soaps became almost synonymous with the type of programme which had been thrown together on a shoe-string budget and which showed up all manner of deficiencies, whether of acting, scripting or technical management. In the early years of television serials, for instance, parts of the flimsy studio sets always appeared to be on the verge of collapsing and the whole soap opera 'world' seemed to be characterized by a distinct lack of solidity. Given the conditions under which soaps were produced and the absence of many of the technical aids now available, it is small wonder that a certain lack of polish showed through. What is far more regrettable is that the myth about soaps' generally shoddy production standards should have persisted for so long and that this label should have been applied so indiscriminately.[4] On occasions one feels that it has been used by critics as a general tactic for devaluing or ridiculing what they see as a highly dubious and addictive form of entertainment.

---

4   One of the favourite targets for this sort of attack was the now-defunct British soap *Crossroads*. For years *Crossroads* was a frequent butt of popular jibes about all manner of supposed shortcomings, to the point where it was sometimes felt that if a stand-up comedian could not raise a laugh by any other means, then cracking a joke at *Crossroads*' expense might.

Producing the goods

The major problem, or rather challenge, that all makers of TV serial drama face is the task of maintaining a high level of productivity in the face of a deadline pressure that is greater than with most other forms of broadcast drama. The necessary output can only be achieved by adopting a broadly industrial mode of production. The production process is accordingly broken down into a chain of separate operations, and individuals or groups are given responsibility for carrying out specific tasks. In this way the making of TV soaps can be likened to other manufacturing processes where each phase of production is routinized to the greatest possible degree.

A considerable number of skills is being mobilized in the course of making a soap opera, but the success of the operation depends on how well all these skills are coordinated. In other words, though certain individuals may be more conspicuous than others, every successful soap remains essentially a team effort. Responsibility for ensuring that all cogs in the production machine function satisfactorily lies with the producer. One person with experience of producing soaps once likened the work to that of a quantity surveyor, in that the producer's main task is that of translating, with a set number of resources, the blueprint which the programme's architects have prepared into a series of finished units: the recorded episodes (Redmond, 1985, p. 39).

The precise powers of the producer will differ according to how the particular company is organized and how the chain of command operates. In the United States, the more one peers into the labyrinthine structure of companies which control soap opera production, the more limited the role of the individual producer seems to be. In Britain producers of TV drama serials appear to have more of a say in the way things are organized and managed, but even so their powers are ultimately constrained by those who have superior positions in the hierarchy: the directors of programmes for the company or the TV drama section chiefs.

The first that a television audience sees or hears about a new soap tends to be in press items or in various forms of publicity put out by the channel itself just prior to the launch of the new programme. As readers will probably be aware, however, this final pre-launch phase is preceded by a long gestation period, often several years in duration, during which a team of workers will have been busily engaged in the many types of planning and preparation which this type of production demands.

Scriptwriting

As might have been anticipated, given the huge popularity of soaps, television companies are constantly being approached – by both established scriptwriters and by non-professionals – with new ideas for soaps. Only a small number of these ideas or outlines is considered viable however, and even those which are acquired with a view to further development, will in all probability have been first offered to several other potential buyers. Phil Redmond, for instance, tells the story of how in 1973 he first came up with the idea for a drama serial to be centred on the lives of residents on a new housing estate. He duly submitted this outline to the five major ITV companies and the BBC, all of whom judged there to be no mileage in the idea. It was not until Channel 4 was set up in 1981 that Redmond found an organization willing to support the project.

In the course of the initial gestation period of a new soap, a number of pilot scripts will have been produced, often by just one or two writers. When the programme moves into full production, however, it is standard practice for a team of writers to be employed, in order to be able to cope with the demands that continuous serial production makes. This is in contrast to the early days of radio soaps where in many cases just one writer handled the script requirements for a daily fifteen-minute show. Scriptwriters, like all other workers involved in the production process, occupy a set position in the organizational hierarchy. One critic with personal experience of producing scripts for soaps, provides the following sobering assessment of scriptwriters' relative importance: 'The writer . . . comes below the script editor or the continuity department, who answer to the associate producer, who is junior to the producer, whose boss is the executive producer, who is employed by the production company, which is owned or controlled or funded by the network or sponsor' (Buckman, 1984, p. 94).

Within the ranks of the writers themselves there is also a hierarchy. There are those who are mainly responsible for determining the general direction which present or future story-lines will take, and those whose principal function it is to translate these broad outlines into scripts for individual episodes. As always, there will be certain company-determined variations as to how different scriptwriting tasks are divided up between those concerned, but in most production teams there is a distinction between those whom we might call the strategic planners with the longer view and those whose job it is to flesh out these basic outlines.

To illustrate how the logistics of scriptwriting are handled in a specific case, one might cite the example of the longest-running soap in existence: *The Guiding Light*. In common with most of the

American daytime soaps *The Guiding Light* is broadcast five times a week and has sixty-minute episodes. There are three 'head writers' attached to the programme whose task it is to come up with what is known as the 'long story'. The story-lines and plot developments covered by the 'long story' are sufficient to carry the programme through the next six months. The head writers also have to supply a 'story calendar' which in the words of one of the show's producers 'gives us a week-by-week listing of emotional and physical events, so that we know where we are by story – not necessarily by individual character, but by story – each week' (Barrett, 1985, p. 37). The next stage in the operation is to pass on the 'long story' to 'breakdown writers' who carve up the narrative in such a way as will conveniently fit into a five-day sequence of episodes. One particular concern is to produce an outline which will accommodate all the commercial breaks (seven per hour!) and end on a tense or intriguing cliff-hanging note to ensure that the audience returns for more on the following Monday.

Once agreement has been reached on these breakdowns (which is usually achieved in collaboration with the show's producers), the outlines are sent to the dialogue writers, who have between a week and ten days to produce their completed scripts. *The Guiding Light* carries a team of five such writers and as the production staff readily admit, the task of turning out this amount of dialogue on such a regular basis can often lead to premature burn-out. With so many writers working on the scripts of different episodes, there are also inevitably certain problems with continuity. In order therefore to ensure that characters continue to use the same sort of language throughout and to avoid any narrative inconsistency, a story editor is employed to pick up all such lapses. Depending on the nature of the changes to be made, one or more of the head writers may again be consulted at this stage and the producer will also have to give his/her seal of approval.

Viewed in this light, working as a dialogue scriptwriter on one of the more popular soaps is a heavily constrained activity. Story contours are clearly marked and much of the landscape detail along the route has already been pencilled in. To some observers this might be – indeed has been – regarded as something of a betrayal of what some claim to be the writer's prerogative, namely to be an inspired begetter of texts. As far as scripting soap opera is concerned, however, it is important that each member of the scriptwriting team resists any temptation to mark the text with the stamp of their own individuality. This not only preserves a sense of continuity, but also maintains the illusion that the whole soap narrative is emanating from an unauthored source.

Directing soaps

What the above description of scriptwriting for soaps makes clear is that the making of a television serial demands a particular discipline from all those involved in the production process. This is no less true of the director, who, like scriptwriters, is usually employed on a fixed-term contract basis when working on a TV soap. In other forms of 'moving image' production, especially in certain types of film-making, the director's contribution will be measured in part by the degree to which the finished product bears the marks of that individual's creative flair. The primary requirement of a TV soap director on the other hand is that such individualistic aspirations are constantly kept in check. It is more a question of discovering and then falling in line with the presentational style and tone which has been developed in the course of the programme's short or long history. As one critic put it: 'Consistency of tone is all-important, even if the tone has to be low' (Buckman, 1984, p. 141).

The main task of the director is to translate the scripts – as produced in the manner outlined above – into the form of episodes ready for transmission. The director's role is thus one which carries with it major responsibility and calls for a range of skills, not the least of which is the ability to extract the best performance out of both actors and technical personnel in situations where rehearsal time is always going to be short. What all directors have to bear in mind is that the majority of the studio staff and the actors they are working with have had in all probability a much longer association with the serial than they have had themselves. Tact, charm, enthusiasm, a fund of relevant experience on which to draw and above all a steady nerve when disaster threatens are all vital prerequisites of being a successful director of soap opera.

With most bi- or tri-weekly soaps the productivity levels which have to be maintained mean that several directors have to be employed simultaneously and given responsibility for a set number of episodes. A typical production schedule for a bi-weekly soap will be geared to a three-week cycle, with, say, three directors in harness, each at a different stage in the cycle. The first two weeks are taken up with final preparations: working through the script and discussing with set designers any special needs for the time spent in the studio. As already noted, recent years have also seen a larger number of scenes shot on location, so one or more location shoots will have to be incorporated into the plan of campaign. The director also has to find time during this fortnight to prepare a *camera script*, which maps out in some detail the shots and camera moves which are best suited to capturing that section of the narrative. The director will also mark on the camera script what movements, actions

```
Sc 8 - Michael approaches Eric       EPISODE 706
and offers him a job.                SCENE NINE
                                     MANSE TEAROOM
     CAMS:  1E, 2J, 4D               10.00 AM


123.  CAM 4                          MORAG SITTING AT A TABLE.
      2S Carol/Morag                 CAROL DELIVERING A POT OF TEA T
                                     HER.   MRS MACK RE-SETTING A
                                     TABLE IN THE BACKGROUND.


                                     CAROL
                                     You're becoming quite a regular
                                     these days.


                                     MORAG
                                     Hardly that.   I was just down
                                     picking up the messages.
                                     Thought I'd drop in for a wee
                                     cuppa.


124.  CAM 1                          MRS ANDERSON HURRIES IN.  /
      L/A LS Hall
      Hold Mrs Anderson to f/g                        (INT. HALL)

      Let Mack into f/g.             MRS ANDERSON
                                     Mrs Mack, Mrs Mack .......


                                     MRS MACK
                                     For heaven's sake, woman, can
                                     you not see I'm busy.


                                     MRS ANDERSON
                                     You'll never guess what I've
                                     just heard.
```

/ 4 NEXT /

and gestures are going to be required of the players.

More than perhaps any other form of television drama production, the directing of soaps necessitates various types of compromise, since there is simply not the time to indulge in lengthy experimentation with what shots work best or to test whether a change in the lighting set-up would bring slightly better results. The consequence of this is that most directors tend to fall back on tried and tested formulae, rather than risk a complicated shot sequence which might add something to the dramatic impact of the scene, but only at the cost of involving everybody in a mad scramble to complete the rest of the episode in the time allotted.

Rehearse and record

The third week of the production cycle is given over to rehearsing and recording. As much as one whole day in this week can be set aside for the outside location scenes. There are then normally two full days of rehearsals. These frequently take place in specially hired rehearsal rooms, where tape markings on the floor indicate the position of certain items to be found on the studio set. This preparative phase is quite important, because in the tightly organized space of the studio it is just as imperative that actors remember their positions as it is they remember their lines. These final rehearsals also give the director the opportunity to make further adjustments to the camera script, since what sometimes appears feasible when plotting things in the mind's eye can often prove to be unworkable when enacted in front of a camera. It is also worth mentioning that actors themselves may have suggestions to make at this stage. It can be the case that certain lines are difficult to deliver, or the actor may pick up on some narrative or character inconsistency which no one else had spotted before that moment.

The latter part of this week – usually at least two full days – is given over to the recording of the rehearsed episodes. Before the final move into the studio, there normally will be a so-called technical run-through, again in the rehearsal room, this time, however, with key members of the studio personnel present. The purpose of this run-through is to check that the rehearsed episodes are viable from the technical point of view and that each episode does not significantly exceed or undercut the prescribed length.

As already suggested, the success of any soap opera depends on the most careful planning and on the well-coordinated efforts of a large number of production workers. The importance of teamwork

What a camera script looks like

Recording a TV soap © **BBC**

is at no time more apparent than during studio days when a wide range of professional skills (acting, technical and production) are being deployed. It is vital therefore that on studio days a good working atmosphere is created in order to achieve maximum efficiency. This calls for considerable managerial as well as diplomatic skills on the part of both director and producer, especially as it involves bringing together what one critic has described as 'two different work cultures in television production' (Hobson, 1982, p. 77): the technical staff who are for the most part studio-bound and the performers who divide their time between rehearsals, location work and studio recording sessions.

Regularly having to set up a studio to record the required number of soap episodes is not only logistically demanding, it is also quite time-consuming. This partly explains why some of the more recent soaps have acquired or had built for them a permanent set. In a conventional TV studio, dressing and lighting the required sets will sometimes take as much as half a day, which means in turn less studio time for performers and crew.

Working practices in the studio vary slightly from soap to soap, depending on how tight the schedule is, but most TV serial productions nowadays adopt the 'rehearse and record' procedure. This simply means that, after some preliminary camera tests, each scene in an episode is rehearsed before being recorded on video tape. It is worth noting, however, that with this approach the scenes are not usually recorded in the order they will eventually occur in the transmitted episode. The reason is the fairly obvious one that it is more efficient to shoot all the scenes scripted for each set one after the other rather than constantly having to switch between different parts of the studio.

Once the studio recordings have been made, the production enters the final editing phase. Though everything possible will have been done to get the timing of individual episodes right at the rehearse/record stage, a certain amount of fine tuning can be done by means of careful editing. An episode which marginally over-runs its allotted time can, for instance, be trimmed to size with comparative ease. More difficult problems arise, however, if the episode under-runs, for it is now too late to take any type of remedial action.

Acting in soaps

From the television public's point of view, the most conspicuous participants in the whole production process are the actors. Because they are so conspicuous – they are literally so often in the public eye – they are especially subject to the kind of sensationalist exposure they frequently get in the popular press.

One result is that the distinction between their personal identity as an actor or actress and that of the character they are playing tends to become progressively more blurred. One might have predicted that – as a result of this blurring – some actors might well develop distinctly schizoid traits. As far as one can judge, however, most actors seem to cope surprisingly well with the pressures that appearing in a long-running soap imposes. Any possible disadvantages (about which more in a moment) tend to be outweighed by the not inconsiderable benefits that being a soap actor can bring. For one thing: acting is a very uncertain profession where at any one time more actors are out of work than are gainfully employed, so getting a part on even a half-way successful soap can mean relative job security. Most soap actors are also able to gain additional income from various forms of promotional activity, made possible by their enhanced status as soap opera personalities. There are of course those who will wish to exploit their 'soap star' status as a way of launching out into another branch of show business entirely (this has recently been a favoured option with several teenage stars who have appeared in Australian soaps).

The kudos that regularly appearing in a TV soap brings should not be allowed to obcure some of the less well-publicized, and possibly more problematical aspects of soap acting. Most performers are, for instance, hired initially on short (often 13-week) contracts, which do not exactly represent secure employment conditions. A long-term involvement with a particular soap can, by contrast, bring problems of a different kind in that the actor concerned becomes so identified with their fictional character that he or she gets virtually straitjacketed within that role. It is for this reason that some actors decide it is in their best interests to sever their connections with the serial in question in order to be able to extend their repertoire of acting roles. It is sometimes possible for soap actors, especially those with minor roles, to take on other forms of TV or film work whilst still being contracted to a particular soap. The pressures of production, however, are such that this type of moonlighting is not all that frequent.

An actor's desire to 'move on' will mean that their character has to be written out of the script, though occasionally it will be decided simply to use another actor in the vacated role. Being written out of a script does not always happen at an actor's request, however. As we have seen, it is the head writers or production chiefs who determine in what way the plot and the various story-lines will develop. If it is decided that the future course of the soap narrative makes certain roles redundant, those characters will be duly jettisoned, using one of the time-honoured devices which writers have fashioned for this purpose: road accident; contracting a terminal illness; emigration; murder or madness. On other occasions it will have been the individual actor who – for a variety of reasons – will have incurred the displeasure of the production chiefs and will be subsequently written out of the script. Almost invariably the 'killing off' of a character will lead to complaints from viewers. If it is a central character who is being forced to depart, there can be a veritable storm of protest. One of the best-known and most highly publicized departures of a character in British soaps was that of Meg Mortimer of *Crossroads*. Meg, played by actress Noelle Gordon, had been the central character in this long-running serial from 1964 until 1981 and for many viewers it was beyond belief that she should be abandoned in this way. For the programme planners on the other hand the future format of the programme counted for more than the audience's long-standing attachment to a character, and in spite of a long campaign to have the character 'saved', the planners eventually had their way.

Meg's departure – like most things in soaps – was not irrevocable, as she made a brief return visit to the programme two years later, but it does point up a general feature of all TV drama serials. This is that no one character (and therefore actor) is absolutely indispensable for the survival of any soap (even though some readers might consider that *Dallas* without JR is practically inconceivable). This has partly to do with one of the distinctive design features of soaps, that – given the constant interweaving of story-lines – audience interest is distributed amongst quite a large number of characters. The other reason is that characters in traditional TV soaps are not, as with certain other forms of drama, created with the physical or temperamental attributes of a particular actor in mind. Characters are developed according to strictly dramatic criteria. This is not to say that actors – especially those in a long-running serial – will not in the course of time to some extent make the character their own by inflecting him or her with some of their own personal idiosyncracies.

Concluding remarks

There is clearly much more that goes into the making of a TV soap opera than it has been possible to include in the above sections. There are, for instance, elaborate promotional campaigns that precede the launch of any new soap and the continuing efforts to maintain a high profile for the programme in the eyes of the viewing public. Television companies – especially in view of the very competitive environment in which they find themselves today – will be continually on the look out for new programme material. Developing a programme from scratch can be a very time-consuming business and the success of the product is by no means guaranteed. The history of soap opera is therefore full of cases where successful manifestations of the genre have been copied or cloned, in an attempt to secure further mileage from a winning formula. Predictably enough – given the fortunes that can be made from a successful soap opera in the United States – some of the best known examples of cloning occur with the American supersoaps.

As television executives and producers continue to seek new ideas, they will be constantly considering how the standard ingredients of soap opera can be freshly blended into a new programme mix. Assessing what is likely to go down well with the current generation of viewers is never an easy task, since audience tastes are notoriously difficult to predict (even with such a popular genre as soaps). It is to the audience and to what they 'make' of soaps that we turn our attention in the next chapter.

4 Watching soaps

It is well known that successful soaps attract large and loyal followings. Over the years this has sometimes led to feverish competition between rival TV channels for the rights to screen programmes which have acquired blockbuster status. One of the most memorable battles in Britain over a rights issue was the squabble in 1985 between Thames Television and the BBC as to who should screen the latest series of *Dallas*. Though soaps have almost always been good news for broadcasters as far as ratings are concerned, they have, as we have seen, been frequently singled out for criticism as a form of down-market programming to which broadcasters will always be tempted to turn as a way of maintaining their audience share. The fear is, in other words, that pressure of competition in an increasingly deregulated broadcasting system will drive out – or at least make it more difficult to sustain – those programmes which have been traditionally associated with quality television, whether this is equated with the probing documentary, the challenging one-off play or with innovative approaches to children's programming. In their place we shall be exposed to an increased number of game shows, quiz programmes and imported soaps, all of which, from the broadcasters' view, combine the twin virtues of being relatively cheap and of making no great demands on their audiences.

The aim of this chapter is to review some of the ways in which TV soap audiences have been traditionally understood and to examine how viewers themselves relate to their favourite soaps. In the past viewers have been cast all too often in the role of mindless consumers of mass-produced entertainment, but on closer inspection – when viewers are encouraged to voice their own opinions about soaps and their meanings – a very different picture emerges. Whilst for many soap watching may well become a consuming passion, there is in fact little evidence to suggest that soaps induce that state of passive, uncritical absorption which no small number of observers would have us believe. On the contrary, what comes through very clearly in the various analyses and surveys which have been conducted into audience response is that the meanings that viewers derive from soaps involve a much more active process of negotiation. Viewers are not just passive recipients or empty vessels into which meanings are poured. Rather, they deploy a whole range of 'decoding' skills and strategies and apply several different frames of reference when engaging with soaps. This means in effect that each person's 'reading' of a TV soap is going to differ from that of his or her neighbour, depending on such factors as the degree of familiarity with the major conventions of the soap genre and the amount of knowledge already possessed of the 'world' of that particular soap.

An active audience

It would be misleading to claim, however, that it is only at the actual point of reception – wherever that may be – that meanings are made. As we have already observed, soaps are constantly being worked over in people's everyday conversations, so what transpires in the course of these exchanges is very much a part of meaning making. In other words, in talking about the significance of soaps, we also have to bear in mind the range of active responses they promote. As Taylor and Mullan have commented: 'People's ability to improvise around the themes and characters of television (gives) the lie to any idea that they merely absorbed, then reproduced, whatever television chose to throw at them' (1987, p. 205).

Conceiving the soap audience as active makers of meaning runs very much counter to earlier views that tended to define the audience in far more monolithic terms as a passive, undifferentiated mass. One reason for the prevalence of this view is that early audience research in the United States was more concerned with establishing how effective programmes such as soaps were at reaching and influencing the large number of potential consumers at whom they were targeted. Few questions were asked about *how* soaps were understood by audiences, nor indeed about the possible differential response on the part of individual 'receivers' (the very use of this term implies passivity). The implicit assumption was that the consumption of soap operas, like other mass media texts, would lead to a series of direct and tangible effects much in the same way that if you injected the body with certain chemical substances a physical reaction would occur.[1]

If audiences for soaps were once thought to be largely passive, they were also considered to be vulnerable. This has meant that, in the relatively short history of soaps, there have been no small number of individuals who have felt it their duty to issue warnings

---

1 In early media research much was made of the 'hypodermic needle' model of communication. The suggestion was that the transfer of a message from sender to receiver could be likened to an injection, as a result of which a discernible change or effect could be registered in the recipient. This all too simplistic model has since been largely discredited.

about the corrupting force of such programmes. One of the earliest attempts to make soaps responsible for a range of social and psychological ills was by a psychiatrist and physician, one Dr Louis I. Berg. Suspecting that several of his female patients who had consulted him about various afflictions, had possibly been exposed to undesirable stimuli, Dr Berg made a three-week study of two of the radio serials which were popular at the time. His findings confirmed all his worst suspicions and enabled him to draw up a list of physiological conditions with which, to his mind, indiscriminate serial consumption was associated. Some indication of how seriously he viewed the matter is given in the following passage from his report: 'Pandering to perversity and playing out destructive conflicts, these serials furnish the same release for the emotionally distorted that is supplied to those who derive satisfaction from a lynching bee, who lick their lips at the salacious scandals of a *crime passionel*', who in the unregretted past cried out in ecstacy at a witch burning' (Thurber, 1949, pp. 251–2).

In these more enlightened times the possibility that soap watchers are laying themselves open to the dangers and diseases which Dr Berg describes have largely been discounted. Yet the idea still persists in some quarters that vulnerable viewers will be adversely affected, if not actually led astray, by what they see and hear. In Britain, for instance, there been has in recent years a vigorous campaign on the part of the National Viewers' and Listeners' Association (NVLA) to articulate what it sees as the 'rights of the audience' to be defended against the allegedly corrupting influence of certain highly popular soaps such as *EastEnders*. The nub of the NVLA argument is that, in the attempt to secure ever higher ratings, broadcasters – in this case the BBC – have exposed viewers to salacious and disturbing material which has no place in that part of the schedule supposedly set aside for 'family viewing'. The claim is that the strong language or violent behaviour in certain scenes goes beyond the limits of what is dramatically necessary and that this could appear to sanction or condone such behaviour, making the assumption that viewers can treat soap characters as role models. In a worst-case scenario therefore, it is alleged that broadcasters could be made at least partly responsible for the increase in certain types of anti-social behaviour.

What Dr Berg and the watchdogs of the NVLA have in common is that both place the viewer in a position of relative impotence. The emphasis is always on the notion of the captivated audience, prey to the manipulation and blandishments of ratings-obsessed broadcasters and advertisers. This is, however, rather a one-sided view of the soap watching experience, and it can be argued that the relationship between a soap and its audience allows for a much greater diversity of response. Indeed one of the reasons why so many people are drawn into long and sometimes heated discussions about soaps is that soap narratives positively encourage more than one interpretation of events. Reduced to a simple formula, this relationship between a soap and its audience is one in which viewers use soaps just as much as they are used by them.

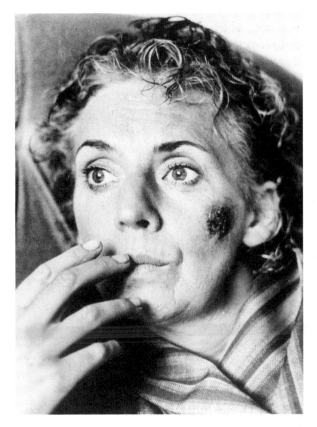

Violence in soaps: Sheila Grant, rape victim in _Brookside_

If, however, we continue to emphasize the notion of the 'active viewer', in what particular ways can this activity be understood? This is a useful point at which to introduce the idea of viewer competence. Each time viewers settle down to watch their favourite soap they are in fact tapping into a whole range of 'reading' skills they have acquired over a span of time. Just as in the reading of words on a page, one will not normally be aware of how much skill is needed to make sense of what one sees on the screen. The more one thinks about it, however, the more skilled an activity it seems to become. It demands not only a general knowledge of the conventions by which soaps operate, but also an ability to mobilize the considerable store of memories and information which constitute the history of this particular soap. All this is involved in being, or becoming, a competent reader of soaps. Only then will one be able to plug in to a veiled hint about trouble brewing for one of the characters. Only then will one be able to discern the irony in a character's apparently innocent remark (because one is able to relate it to a much earlier event).[2]

Soap in the home. . .

The circumstances in which soaps are viewed are plainly going to have some impact on how they are 'read' and understood by audiences. It is only comparatively recently, however, that studies have been published which give us a clearer idea of how audiences react and behave while watching soaps. These studies have caused us once again to revise some of the distortions or mistaken assumptions about audience response. In this section we shall be considering the implications of these findings for how audiences relate to television soaps (see especially Morley, 1986, and Taylor and Mullan, 1987).

One fondly cherished notion which these audience-orientated research surveys have effectively demolished is that there is any such thing as a typical viewer. Indeed the traditional image of an isolated chair- or sofa-bound individual sitting in a semi-darkened room transfixed by the flickering screen has now largely given way to a much more differentiated view of the audience, one in which the act of viewing is seen as much a social, as it is an individual, activity. This is of course a reflection of the fact that the domestic environment in which most TV viewing occurs is one in which single-minded devotion to the screen (even if this were desirable) is precluded by a range of other activities which are taking place simultaneously. Just as with other forms of TV programming, soaps have in a sense to compete with these other family and domestic activities. As David Morley has astutely observed: '"Watching television" cannot be assumed to be a one-dimensional activity which has equivalent meaning or significance at all times for all who perform it' (1986, p. 15). The fact that soaps are frequently watched in the company of others, most of whom know each other very well, immediately sets up the possibility of various forms of exchange.

---

2   One gets some idea of just how much competence many viewers of soaps have acquired by considering the example of *Hollywood Sports*, (see p. 14–15), where viewer competence was clearly sufficient to allow many viewers to become active collaborators in the production process.

For some viewers, being forced to listen to a stream of often disparaging comments can be extremely irritating, but for others the possibility of participating in this way constitutes one of the pleasures of soap viewing.

In assessing audience response to television soaps then, one cannot – for the reasons outlined – always presuppose a high level of sustained concentration. Soap watching for some viewers can indeed become a secondary or complementary activity. It can be accommodated amongst a series of other household or family tasks and pursuits and is not something to which one necessarily has to give one's full attention. Intermittent glances at the screen and keeping one ear tuned in to the dialogue will normally suffice to keep abreast of important narrative developments.

Soaps meet their viewers more than half-way in aiding and abetting this form of distracted viewing. Plots do not move ahead at breakneck speed and the fact that viewers are normally familiar with the broad contours of a story-line makes it relatively easy for them to be kept in the picture, even if they do miss some of the action. Scriptwriters also ensure that important plot developments are introduced in such a way that they will be the subject of comment by several characters in the course of more than one episode. This has the additional advantage that viewers who have missed out on the occasional episode – almost inevitable in the life of a long-running soap – can easily catch up. There are also certain agencies which provide a support service to viewers in this respect. The American publication *The Soap Opera Digest* gives synopses of the story-lines of all the major network soaps, whilst various other companies put out similar information via a dial-a-soap telephone service. All this means that what many sharp-tongued critics see as a lamentable deficiency in soaps – the frequent repetition and the painfully slow narrative development – is from the point of view of many in the audience a particular virtue in that it enables viewers to continue their relationship with the programme in spite of temporary separation.

In discussing the type of viewing behaviour most associated with soap watching, one should not conclude that all soap operas are the same in the sort of demands they make on audience attention. (As we shall see in the following section, viewers relate to soaps in a variety of different ways, depending as much on what they want to get out of the programme as what is put in by the programme producer.) Broadly speaking, however, those soaps whose lineage can be traced back directly to the daytime radio serials of the 1930s will display a number of those features which allow for forms of

Violence in soaps: Ken Barlow and Mike Baldwin come to blows in *Coronation Street*

easy or distracted viewing.[3] The faster moving, action-packed TV soaps which have come on stream in the last decade or two and which tend to feature rapid switches of scene and location, arguably make more demands on viewer attention; although studies of actual audience reactions again show the same diversity of response as one finds with more traditional soaps. Thus, whilst with programmes like *Dallas* and *Dynasty* there will be some viewers who settle down to enjoy them as pure escapist entertainment in the way they would an adventure yarn or a piece of romantic fiction, there will be others who view the rapid sequence of melodramatic events with a mixture of humour, irony and detachment. For these viewers, the relative modesty of their own home environment is in such contrast to the glossy fictional extravaganzas, that part of the pleasure of viewing can lie in the opportunities for making ironic comments on how far removed this world is from that of their own lived experience.

Whilst the supersoaps will – for the most part – always point up the contrast between the glossy fictional world and the more mundane world in which viewers themselves are situated, the more

3　One contention is that this aspect of soaps' form and structure was developed so that women – the prime target audience – could more easily integrate soaps into their various domestic duties.

traditional daytime soaps tend, if anything, to have the opposite effect. This is especially the case with those soaps in the *Coronation Street* tradition that aspire to a high degree of social realism in their narrative accounts of supposedly everyday life. With these soaps there is frequently a fairly close parallel between the fictional world of the serial and the everyday world into which the pictures flow. This resemblance between the two domains is one of the reasons why many viewers develop such a strong sense of identification with soap characters and the places they inhabit. It is as if the fictional world simply becomes an extension of their own and one into which they can move with greater ease than Alice passing through the looking-glass.

Uses and gratifications of soap watching

One of the other main findings to emerge out of the body of research into how audiences make sense of soaps is that individual viewers seem able to respond on various different levels. For instance, there are no small number of viewers who at one level find it easy to suspend their disbelief and to become totally absorbed in what they see and hear, whilst at another level being well aware of all the artifice that goes into a soap's construction. To express the same point in slightly different terms: soaps have the capacity to create forms of involvement seldom paralleled in other types of dramatic fiction, but at the same time offer the possibility of more playful, ironically detached responses which keep everything at one remove from our world and allow us to treat the whole thing as an elaborate, but enjoyable game.

A more fruitful approach to the question of what impact soaps, have on audiences is to continue to focus attention on the diversity of viewer response and to discover more about the range of pleasures which are most commonly associated with soap watching. In the following sections therefore we shall attempt to chronicle the reasons viewers give for continuing to watch TV serials and to draw attention to the particular 'needs' that these fictions seem to be fulfilling or gratifying.[4]

---

4   The so-called 'Uses and Gratifications' theory suggests that an audience response to a media text is determined by how that text meets or gratifies a particular and often complex set of needs. The theory has sometimes been criticized because it tends to underestimate how messages can be presented in such a way as to make it more likely that a certain 'reading' will be forthcoming in spite of gratification being sought.

A regular encounter

One of the most salient features of soaps – and one which many would say lies at the heart of their appeal – is that they provide a regular source of entertainment. The consequence of this is that for many viewers the time allotted to their favourite soap becomes an integral part of their personal and domestic routine. Other activities and obligations are planned in such a way to accommodate the various soap-watching slots. Some people regard their regular soap appointment as a well-deserved reward for the various types of toil in which they have been otherwise engaged, although there are some viewers who become afflicted with guilty feelings that this 'habit' is causing them to neglect what some might regard as less trivial pursuits.

The knowledge that viewers are ready to fit at least part of their everyday lives around soaps has led television broadcasters to pay close attention to the scheduling of these programmes. Much thought is given to the slot in the schedule a new soap will occupy, since this will clearly determine the type and the size of the audience which can be expected. One of the several assumptions which TV schedulers make about the audience for traditional soaps is that viewers will be more likely to be able to make a regular viewing commitment during the week than at weekends, when it is presumed people are less tied to their home base. Needless to say, schedulers and broadcasters also keep a watchful eye on what is happening on rival channels and any move in the presentational pattern of one soap almost always leads to a response from the 'competition'. In Britain, for instance, we have in recent years witnessed a growing number of weekend omnibus editions of the major soaps, as broadcasters seek to provide the opportunity for viewers who have missed an episode or two to make good that loss.

As one of the special appeals of soaps is the ease with which they can be integrated into the rhythms and patterns of domestic or workaday life, any decision affecting the timing of transmission is never taken lightly. The producers of Scottish Television's bi-weekly serial *Take the High Road* were more than a little concerned about possible adverse reaction to the decision that the Monday episode should go out at a different time in the early evening schedule than the episode later in the week. (Both episodes now have the same starting-time.) Likewise it was only after considerable audience research that Granada Television took the momentous decision to screen three rather than two episodes of *Coronation Street* a week. (The claim was that many viewers regarded the interval between the Wednesday and the following Monday episodes as too long a period of time, even allowing for the fact that part of the enjoyment of every soap opera lies in the pleasurable anticipation of the next encounter).

A launch-pad for social and personal interaction?

Regular followers of soaps are not just individual consumers. They also share their fascination with a very much larger audience. One of the pleasures of soap watching therefore is the opportunity it provides for exchanging views with others on a variety of issues ranging from a character's dress-sense to how implausible a new story-line may be. In this sense soaps can justifiably be regarded as an aid to social interaction. Viewers evidently not only know a lot about soaps, they get a great deal of enjoyment from sharing this knowledge with kindred souls, whether these be family and friends or total strangers. The precise purpose which underlies this sharing of knowledge will differ according to the situation. In some cases it will be used as an 'ice-breaking' ploy to get a conversation moving (as an alternative to talking about the weather!). At other times, by commenting on the stance taken by a particular character over a certain matter, viewers are able to broach issues which they might otherwise have found very difficult to talk about. In this respect we would agree with those who claim that soaps provide a launch-pad for people to explore aspects of their own lives and value systems by relating and comparing, say, the moral dilemmas and problems faced by characters in a soap to their own particular circumstances (see especially Livingstone, 1988, pp. 55–80).

Thus, far from being an activity which stifles conversation and which isolates people from one another, soap watching – especially in a group or family environment – can positively promote a variety of communicative activities, ranging from occasional interjections to more extended post-programme debates. In the eyes of some researchers these exchanges highlight a further use of soap watching. Namely it encourages a sense of cohesion and togetherness, which in earlier times was associated with such pursuits as card-playing and music-making, in an age when individuals are suffering increasingly from feelings of alienation. Gathering in front of the screen for the next episode of the 'family' soap can, in other words, take on something of the quality of a uniting ritual.

Fulfilling person-centred needs?

Whilst soaps may help in promoting various forms of communicative exchange, they can also be seen as serving an altogether different set of needs. In broad terms these are what we might describe as 'person-centred', in that they have more to do with the pleasure and enjoyment that individual viewers hope to get out of the soap-watching experience. This can often lead to a particularly strong sense of identification with the soap in question, to the point that the person concerned will wish to view the programme alone rather than risk the possibility of others moving in on their domain. To these ends certain viewers will go to considerable lengths to mark off a space which they alone intend to occupy. In the family viewing situation this can lead to various types of skirmishing concerning, for instance, who should have charge of the remote control device or who can be relied upon not to sabotage the programme by a stream of uncalled-for comments (the assumption being that a respectful silence should be observed).[5]

For many viewers, however, the fear of encroachment does not arise, because they are already living alone. This leads us to comment on another category of need which soaps fulfil. They appear, namely to have a compensatory function. For those living in conditions of social isolation, the regular encounter with their favourite soap can be regarded as providing some measure of compensation for the loneliness which might otherwise be more difficult to endure. In this respect characters in soaps can – in a very real sense – become companions, and viewers can involve themselves in the lives of these characters as if they were family friends. For the lonely and isolated then, the forms of involvement made possible by soaps provide a strong sense of reassurance.

Identification and involvement
When asked to define the special pleasures which soap watching brings, most viewers make some reference to the relationships they are able to form with soap characters. Almost all film and television narratives will encourage some form of identification between the audience and the fictional characters, but there is evidence to suggest that many soap viewers enter into a relationship which is of a very different order. The reasons for this are fairly obvious: no other genre allows the same sustained contact with characters as soaps. It is this long-term involvement which enables viewers to establish a sense of intimacy with certain characters which may be wholly lacking in their day-to-day lives. And what can lend a particular poignancy to these relationships is that the characters – over a span of years – visibly age or mature in the same way as the viewers themselves.

---

5   This type of skirmishing has become somewhat rarer, since increased multi-set ownership and wider access to video-recorders now make it possible for individuals to view 'their' programme at times or in places where they will not be disturbed.

The degree of attachment or type of involvement will vary from viewer to viewer of course, and will be dependent on a number of factors. It is possible, however, to make certain broad distinctions between different types of relationship. One fairly recent investigation, for example, used a graded scale to quantify the nature and intensity of viewer involvement. The results of the survey confirmed that most viewers were indeed drawn into a relationship with characters and that in broad terms they distinguished between those characters to whom they simply felt able to relate and those with whom they could positively identify. As one of the respondents in the survey put it:

> It is possible to identify with many of the characters, to see families on screen suffering traumas, going through happy times, illness, bereavement and all the situations that combine to make up life, it gives you a feeling of belonging, of not being the only one that has to face up to the everyday tensions (Livingstone, 1988, p. 71).

The soap audience's capacity for empathy and identification means that viewers feel especially close to characters when the latter are going through times of stress, drama or crisis, situations which are not all that infrequent in the world of soap opera. The degree of involvment is such that one might even suggest that viewers – in the grip of such feelings – are undergoing a form of catharsis. In so far as catharsis provides a positive outlet for the channelling of pent-up emotions, one could arguably claim that some viewers derive therapeutic benefit from this harmless form of emotional indulgence.

Escapist fantasy?

In many people's estimation soaps provide a form of entertainment which primarily caters for viewers' escapist needs. The contention is that viewers use soaps to detach themselves from the worries and concerns of everyday life and immerse themselves in a fictional world, whether this be the plush, oil-rich surroundings of a Texan ranch or the humbler, working-class setting of a Northern industrial town. Some viewers clearly regard the ability of soaps to transport them out of their own worlds as a major part of the genre's continuing appeal. (Perhaps we should recall here Sir John Betjeman's words about regularly visiting paradise!)

Whilst most soaps resemble other forms of fiction in that they provide an alternative reality which viewers can safely occupy without fear of recrimination, some soaps contain a stronger fantasy element than others. This is especially true of the American super-soaps, part of whose attraction is that they are 'out of this world'.

As one woman in a recent audience survey commented: 'That's what's nice about it [*Dynasty*]. It's a dream world, isn't it' (Morley, 1986, p. 165). The appeal of the supersoaps therefore is that viewers feel they are literally being taken out of themselves and being allowed access to a glittering and glamorous world far removed from their own. (There is an analogy here between the way an audience views notable characters in soaps and how they relate to members of the royal family.)

For no small number of viewers the experience of watching some of the more fantastical and melodramatic soaps is not unlike that of reading or listening to fairy tales, which are also marked by a strong contrast between two levels of reality. The fairy tale analogy is also applicable in another sense. Fairy tales, it is generally agreed, play through at an imaginative level many of the central conflicts or dramas of the human condition: the struggle between the forces of good and evil, the secret desires which lie below the 'civilized' surface of life. Likewise soaps – and especially the supersoaps where the melodramatic impulse is strongest – have the ability to connect with parts of our fantasy lives that other fictions may not be able to reach (see Ang, 1982).

Learning from soaps

Soap watching does not just involve being pleasurably absorbed in a fictional world, thus serving what are essentially escapist needs. Viewers also look to soaps – especially those which belong to the traditional category – to provide a fictionalized account of problems and conflicts which are much closer to home than the wilder antics of the heroes and villains of the supersoaps. As we shall discover in the following chapter, the traditional soaps' continuing concern with what appear to be some of the more pressing everyday problems of life has always enhanced their claim to be thought of as realistic. The early American daytime soaps, for instance, which were aimed almost exclusively at an audience of housewives, often focused on typical difficulties faced by women in the home and offered advice on how to cope with both domestic and emotional problems. As soaps developed, however, they became less prone to adopt a didactic or counselling stance *per se*, and any 'messages' that were introduced were embedded in the narrative in such a way that they had rather to be deduced by the reader than being explicitly spelled out in the text.

What soaps therefore provide are a number of possibilities for learning (in the widest sense of the word) about a range of contemporary problems. Not all of these are directly relevant to viewers' own lives and relationships, but they are normally issues on which they might nevertheless be expected to have a view. Sometimes the learning takes the form of viewers discussing among themselves the rights and wrongs of a course of action which a character in a soap is taking and, in the process, discovering more about how they stand on that particular issue. These discussions – as to how a dilemma can be resolved or a rift healed – are often pursued with some intensity, since viewers frequently feel deeply implicated in the lives of the characters. It is almost as if the efforts to find an appropriate solution are being undertaken in the conviction that advice on what action to take can be communicated to the parties involved.

Whilst there is every justification for claiming that viewers derive certain 'educational' benefits from mulling over the 'real life' issues which are incorporated into soap narratives, one must also put these claims in perspective. As already suggested, soaps are primarily conceived as dramatic entertainments, so any attempt to make them too problem-orientated can be counter-productive if audiences sense in any way that they are being lectured to. This means that when it comes to deciding what issues are to be dealt with in soap story-lines, the major consideration is always in what way it will enhance the narrative appeal of the programme. It is for this reason that TV soap producers turn down the majority of requests they get from 'socially responsible' organizations – or even government agencies – to work a particular issue into a future story-line as part of a publicity or consciousness-raising exercise. As a former executive producer of *Coronation Street* put it: 'We rarely react to these unsolicited requests, unless we feel that we can introduce a dramatic story illustrating the situation' (Podmore, 1984, p. 12).

Soaps in other words do not aspire to being pseudo-documentaries, in spite of their treatment of a range of contemporary issues. Soaps are also prevented – by the narrative and other conventions under which they operate – from taking up a polemical or politically progressive stance on the various issues which they broach. For instance, most of the problems which traditional soaps have chosen to deal with over the years have been confined to the private or domestic sphere. The wider sphere of public, political and industrial affairs has been in effect off-limits for soaps, with the notable exception of *Brookside*. This has meant that when social problems have been introduced into the narrative, they are almost always reduced to the personal dimensions of a particular case, as opposed to being seen, say, in a larger economic framework. This has led some critics to express the concern that, far from being potentially educative, soaps might encourage the unwarranted belief that all problems are somehow 'people related' (Cantor and Pingree, 1983, p. 137). Such views – it has to be said – rest on the questionable

assumption that audiences are easily duped into accepting all they
see and hear, and discounts or underestimates their ability to apply
their own frames of reference.

Therefore, in spite of having a certain educative appeal, soaps do
not in the final analysis aspire to being pseudo-documentaries. They
remain primarily entertainments, although in the process of being
diverted viewers may also discover they are being given considerable
food for thought and reflection. The hope is that, by taking socially
or politically relevant issues, one will be able, in the words of one
producer 'to balance the dramatic requirements of modern, small-
screen entertainment with a real sense of depth, concern and insight'
(Redmond, 1987, p. 9).

Dear Sir,

"TAKE THE HIGH ROAD"

    Thankyou for your letter of 1st. March: In it you refer to a new series of
"Take The High Road", but so far, now four weeks later, I have not been aware of
any great change; except that is, that this month the episodes have been better
than usual and, coincidently have answered some of the points which I raised.

    My first point was the issue of "Isabel" and the council elections. I
was pleasantly surprised to find this matter re-introduced and that more will come
of it this time.

    The second point I raised concerned "Mark Ritchie", or the lack of him!
It has been gratifying therefore to see him featured more often recently as both
this charachter and the actor taking the part are very interesting. Long may
this continue! It is also a bonus to east coast ears to hear a Scottish accent
other than the Glasgow/west coast one, which on the 'box' in general, seems to
be dominant.

    Regarding the other charachter which I mentioned ie. "Sneddon", I cannot
say that I am happy that he seems destined to go. This charachter to my mind
is a mainstay in the series and Derek Lord fits the part of the 'handsome nasty'
superbly. His absence will leave a gap and many disappointed fans.

    Reading the credits each week where the writers seem to frequently change,
reminds me of the childrens' game, when one person writes a sentence at the top of
the page, hides it by turning the paper over and the next person has to continue
with another sentence starting with the last word of the former, and so on.
Perhaps this is the weakness of the present series in that one writer following
on another does not have the feeling for the charachters created by the first,
with the subsequent effect that some charachters have unbelievable personality
changes which leave the vier bemused.

    "T.T.H.R." has such a good basis which is unique to other 'soaps' ie. -
a Scottish country community, that with just a little more sophistication in the
planning, but still keeping the Scottish charachter, it could be really something!

Yours sincerely,

A reader's letter to producers of *Take the High Road*

Soap watching as a form of game

Some members of the audience clearly do derive pleasure from suspending their belief and losing themselves in the soap opera world. There is, however, evidence to suggest that one of the other gratifications which soaps can provide is associated not so much with being absorbed as with maintaining a critical, and often ironic distance. To be more specific, one level of audience appreciation of soaps involves focusing attention on the various mechanisms by which they work and in effect pitting one's wits against those of the originating team as to what further narrative developments are possible given the present configuration of characters and story-lines. For these viewers the particular gratification of soaps lies in imagining that they are co-authors in the programmes' construction. The pleasure is almost equivalent to that of the chess-player in that one is trying to work out what moves are possible with the pieces or characters placed as they are.

This form of soap watching presupposes considerable familiarity with the rules and conventions of the soap opera genre. Some research suggests that such an attitude of ironic detachment is more often found in those countries where soap opera entertainment has been almost as freely available as tap water. For these viewers soap watching does not require their full and undivided attention, but is something they can dip into and out of as the mood moves them. As Taylor and Mullan comment: 'Some groups in our society certainly seem able to take or leave soap opera, flicking the dramas on and off as the spirit takes them, . . . commenting on the predictability of it all, precluding any emotional response of their own by erecting a large kitsch bracket around the entire period of viewing' (1987, p. 120).

Concluding remarks

In writing about the variations in the way people watch soaps, one is bound to remark that individual viewers cannot simply be slotted in to one of these categories. This would be tantamount to suggesting that individuals could opt for a different style of viewing according to whether it was the Monday or the Friday episode. As we have seen, motivations for watching can be quite complex and likewise the pleasures or gratifications which soaps afford can be both variable and multi-faceted. There are viewers who will be more inclined to believe in the reality of the world evoked by the soap and who will respond accordingly. Equally there will continue to be those who gain their pleasure from a more detached and critical style of viewing. For a considerable number of viewers, however, these different styles or modes of viewing will not be seen as mutually exclusive. Indeed the very possibility of being able to apply more than one frame of reference in responding to the programme might be regarded as a particularly attractive feature of soap watching. All in all, it would seem almost inevitable that individuals over a period of time could well go through a series of phases during which they employ different strategies in their approach to – and gain different pleasures from – the experience of soap watching.

5 The realism of soaps

One of the criteria most often used by critics and viewers in measuring the impact of soaps is how realistic they appear to be. In the early days of radio soaps, for instance, a recurrent complaint was that the world evoked in these stories was one which seemed totally detached from the everyday lives of their listeners. In James Thurber's words: 'Many a soap town appears to have no policemen, mailmen, milkmen, storekeepers, lawyers, ministers or even neighbours. The people live their continually troubled lives within a socio-economic structure which only faintly resembles our own' (Thurber, 1949, p. 210). The explanation that Thurber gives for these 'soap towns' not being recognizable as 'realistic communities' nor their inhabitants identifiable as 'authentic human beings' is that the housewife-listeners for whom these programmes were intended would not have been attracted by attempts at slice-of-life realism, which would simply remind them of situations and experiences of which they were already painfully aware. What they were looking for were more escapist forms of melodramatic entertainment, in the course of which they could – in Thurber's phrase – 'lose (themselves) in the trials and tribulations, the emotional agonies and soul searchings of the good women in the serials' (ibid. p. 211).

Whilst not denying that certain modern soaps are not without their melodramatic moments, most people would agree that the picture has changed somewhat since Thurber's times. Traditional soaps have developed additional strategies for engaging an audience's attention, with the result that both in what they depict and how they depict it, many soaps now lay claim to a greater measure of realism. However, the difficulty still remains of providing an adequate explanation of their 'greater realism'. What then is the nature of this realism and in what ways can it be understood?

How real are soaps?

As fictional representations soaps do not set out – as has already been suggested – to provide a documentary account of situations and events, but seek rather to create the illusion of a reality. In this respect they may be regarded as belonging to that much larger tradition in art, literature and the theatre to create in the mind of the viewer or reader the impression that what is being evoked is in some sense 'real'. In using the term 'real' in this way, one is suggesting that the work in question is copying – more or less faithfully – some aspect of reality or is communicating a sense of lived experience. In the case of soaps, so the argument goes, the realism effect can be particularly strong, and this in itself may go some way to explaining the potency of their appeal.

The particular feature of soaps which possibly contributes to the realism effect above all else is their explicit or implicit claim to create what has variously been called a 'pseudo reality' or a 'parallel world'. In the words of one American critic:

> It (soap opera) offers itself to its audience as the representation of lives that are separate from but continuous with their own . . . Through the very power of continuity it suggests a kind of heightened realism that is further reinforced by an apparent absence of the kind of compact dramatic patterning associated with traditional theater or cinema (Newcomb, 1979, p. 88).

Using these criteria one measures the realism quotient of soaps by the extent to which they provide a plausible and credible account of the everyday lived experience of individuals. Because many of the activities we see them engaged in are of the humdrum domestic or family-centred variety familiar to most of us, this sense of a 'parallel world' is often quite strong. To these ends producers and writers of soaps will go to considerable lengths to ensure that the decor and the look of houses, hostelries and streets is accurate and conforms to audience expectations about the items one would typically find in such settings.

Accuracy of detail and a concern to emphasize something of the ordinariness of life is one way in which traditional soaps enhance their claim to be realistic. There is another sense in which soaps aspire to be labelled realist. This has to do with the wider question of how faithfully soaps reflect certain aspects of the social and political realities of the times. The relationship and relevance of soaps to contemporary realities has been at the centre of much lively debate, particularly since opinions as to what is 'relevant', – and even to what is constituted by 'reality' – are subject to widely different interpretations. Suffice it to say that each soap will have to negotiate its own stance on the precise way in which it seeks to persuade the audience that it is in tune with the times, through what issues it explores, what contemporary references it introduces and what attitudes the characters display.

Being in tune with the times has also meant that each longer-running soap has had to adjust itself to mirror at least some of the changes which have occurred in the wider society. The extent of the mirroring will again be subject to wide variation from soap to soap and much will depend whether the changes relate to mere surface realities (clothes and outward appearances) or something rather more fundamental (social attitudes and beliefs). If one takes the view that some soaps are responsive to such changes, they can thus be seen as throwing some light on how a particular society or culture attempts to represent itself to itself. In other words, soaps have an ideological significance. A good example of an ideological reading of a contemporary British soap is provided by the following reflections on *Coronation Street* by the senior Labour Party politican Roy Hattersley. Looking back over the last two decades, he observes that for him *Coronation Street* has projected a telling image of significant shifts in social attitudes. In his words:

> *Coronation Street* may not influence the nation's conduct, but it is a reflection of the country's behaviour . . . Twenty years ago, four out of five episodes of *Coronation Street* ended in a way which made me feel more hopeful about the world than I did when the programme began. Now, the feel-good ratio is down to no more than 50 per cent. And being depressed by *Coronation Street* depresses me in general. For I fear that, just as it mirrors changes in the social composition of society, it may also provide a more or less accurate reflection of the change from optimism to cynicism, which is characteristic of the last two decades (*Guardian*, 13 January 1990).

The realism of domestic settings

Realism – in the eye of the beholder

The degree to which soaps are considered realistic not only hinges on what subjects are incorporated into soap texts and how these issues are treated, it will also depend in no small measure on what audiences themselves bring to soaps. Familiarity with some of the topographic detail in soaps will, for instance, often enhance the sense of realism. In the previous chapter we have drawn attention to the active role of audiences and the range of 'skills' they bring to bear in making sense of soap dramas. As we saw, certain intrinsic characteristics of the soap opera text together with quite wide differences in audience composition encourage markedly different responses and interpretations. This differential audience response also has to be borne in mind when discussing the issue of realism. There will be some viewers who will want to compare what they see and hear against their own 'real-life' experience and concerns, whilst there will be others who delight in all those attributes of soaps which mark them as works of fiction. Or, perhaps more accurately, the same viewer is capable at certain times of according a 'reality status' to what he or she sees, whilst at others is moved to adopt a far more critical stance.[1]

A slightly different approach to the question of how realistic or otherwise soaps appear to be involves introducing the notion of coding. The argument, in a nutshell, is that soaps are comparatively 'open' texts and the reason why they lend themselves to such diverse and sometimes contradictory responses is that they contain several different 'codes'. What happens at the moment that soap meets viewer is that these codes are activated and meanings begin to be made. In the words of the critic Robert Allen, this is: 'a complex exchange in which a number of distinct codes engage the reader in the interpretive process' (Allen, 1983, p. 101). The codes referred to can be broadly divided up between those which have a reality orientation and those which underline the fictional status of the work. Soaps are not radically different from other fictional texts in this respect, but where they do differ is in the degree of *slippage* which occurs between these codes. As Allen comments: 'The soap opera consciously walks the line between texts that can be read as fiction and those which, for various reasons, constantly spill over in to the experiential world of the viewer, as few, if any, other fictions do' (ibid. p. 105).

---

1   Critics have used various terms to describe this distinction. Liebes and Katz (1986) suggest that viewers assign meanings to soaps a) by applying a 'referential' framing (i.e. they relate events in the soap directly to those in real life) and b) by adopting a more 'critical' framing (i.e. they take a more detached and distanced view of the narrative).

Moving inside and outside the text

Most viewers, when asked 'How real do you think soaps are?' or 'How realistic do you find soaps?' will not respond by referring to the various codes which are determining their interpretation. When one examines some of the research projects or surveys in which viewers are asked to reflect on their response to soaps, essentially the same points about *slippage* are made, even though different terminology is used. In one such project aimed at establishing what relationship viewers cultivated with the BBC soap *EastEnders*, the researcher was struck by the apparent ease with which the young-sters he was interviewing appeared to move inside and outside the text. In his own words: 'What is interesting is the way they con-stantly shift back and forth between two positions – at certain points they appear to be judging the programme from *outside* the fictional world, while at others they seem to accept the reality of that world, and make their judgements, as it were, from *inside* it' (Buckingham, 1987, p. 172).

Nowhere is the capacity to shift positions outside and inside the text more clearly apparent than over the issue of characters about to be written out of the script. At such times many in the soap audience first recognize the depth of attachment they feel for a character (even for the villains of the piece!), to the extent that the prospect of their imminent departure can fill viewers with a sense of consider-able apprehension. It is as if we only become aware of what some-thing means to us when there is a possibility we will lose it or be denied access. With characters about to be killed off, viewers fre-quently experience a tug of emotions in which there will be on the one hand feelings of, say, sadness or regret, and on the other irri-tation or even anger that such a move has been decided by anony-mous TV executives without taking the reactions of the public sufficiently into account.

Viewed from inside the text, it is as if one were faced with an impending bereavement, whilst from outside the text there is an equally clear recognition that all soap characters are in fact fictional creations and that therefore everything which is set to happen can be changed at the production team's behest. With long-standing characters, however, it is undeniable that – whether threatened with extinction or not – they become in the eyes of many viewers a genuine 'living presence'. What lies behind this relationship is explored in the following section.

A reality born of familiarity?

In the eyes of many observers, the reality status which soaps acquire results largely from viewers' regular and sustained exposure to a world with which they become increasingly more familiar. Having regular access to a world, the contours of which soon take on the quality of a second home, can for many viewers be a deeply reassuring and pleasurable experience, as they get the impression that they are in some way extending their own horizons in the process. The fact that viewers are constantly being drawn back to fictional homes and localities which are instantly recognizable can also lend additional credibility and make it more likely that viewers will be ready to suspend their disbelief. The underlying psychology of this is that one is more inclined to believe in what one sees if one is already reasonably familiar with the context in which certain actions are going to take place and with the personalities involved. (By the same token, the content of items in TV news broadcasts is partly authenticated by the fact that viewers become so familiar with newscasters.)

Resident gossips and busybodies: Mrs Mack in *Take the High Road*

One of the other results of this familiarity is that viewers build up a store of knowledge of the soap opera world which makes it seem in some respects more real than the one they actually inhabit. In the eyes of some critics this is yet further proof that soaps are not only escapist, but dangerously so. What these critics overlook, however, is that becoming temporarily absorbed in a fictional world is not synonymous with losing control of one's critical faculties. The fascination is not mindless; it stems as often as not from long-term involvement and interest. Far from lapping up all that producers and scriptwriters set before them, viewers are very sensitive to the introduction of anything which could mar the credibility and plausibility of the soap narrative. They are, for instance, particularly good at spotting inconsistencies or mistakes in continuity.

Dramas of everyday life

Even though soaps contain incidents and happenings that will occasionally – and in the case of the supersoaps frequently – stretch the credulity of the audience, the fact that we are so intimately acquainted with the characters and their surrounds is likely to enhance the reality status of what we see.

There can be no doubt that one of traditional soaps' lasting appeals is the way they register and reflect some of the more mundane realities of life. One of the pleasures of soap watching is thus being able to spot traces and echoes of our everyday lives in the fictional events we allow to flow into our domestic space. The events referred to here are those which are the subject of many real-life conversations, namely the progress of relationships, the viability of people's plans, the problems certain families are going through – and much more besides. What seems to give soap dialogues a peculiarly authentic ring or appeal is the fact that so many of the exchanges focus on revelations and conjecture about other people. In plainer English, they centre on gossip. In the words of one observer: 'for the committed viewer, part of the enjoyment is the assimilation of the fictional world into everyday life . . . There is special pleasure in letting the ephemera of other communities spill into our own sitting rooms . . . Soap operas are tailor-made forgossip because of the accessibility of their worlds' (Root, 1986, p. 46).

It would be no exaggeration to say that one of the major driving-forces in soap narratives is gossip. In this respect soaps do not so much pander to our escapist tendencies as appeal to that less endearing side of human nature to speculate on what others are doing or thinking, frequently regardless of whether this has any foundation in fact. As was suggested in a previous chapter (see p. 43–5), soaps are especially well adapted to this trading in gossip, since we are constantly being switched between story-lines much in the same way that gossips will range over two or three subjects in the course of a single information-exchange period. Soaps also normally have their own resident gossip or busybody whom audiences specifically associate with the spreading of rumours or poking their nose into other people's business.

Whilst the prevalence of gossip in soaps gives audiences the sense of real-life experience being communicated, there is also the important question of where an audience is placed to witness these revelations. As with other types of film or television fiction, the audience is always conveniently placed *vis-à-vis* the drama that is being played out. This casts the viewers in the role of eavesdropper or even voyeur, since they are enabled to take up the position of silent, unseen witness as characters unburden themselves of some of their most private thoughts and feelings. Witnessing events in this way can reinforce not only an audience's sense of identification and involvement, but also the reality status of what is being witnessed.

A sense of time and a sense of place

Most traditional soaps encourage us to believe that what is being enacted is unfolding in 'real time'. This is in marked contrast to other forms of film or television fiction where time frequently seems

Resident gossips and busybodies: Ena, Martha and Minnie in the early days of
Coronation Street

to rush by at quite a breathless pace. In soaps, however, time moves forward at a pace which we feel is more in keeping with our subjective sense of time passing. By creating the illusion that time in the fictional world is running in step with the viewers' own time, the sense of a 'parallel world' is reinforced. By allowing stories to develop at what sometimes seems to be a decidedly leisurely tempo, soaps further enhance their claim to be thought of as realistic.

The slow narrative progression of soaps is partly attributable to the characteristic interweaving of story-lines. This constant switching of focus gives the impression of much happening simultaneously in the lives of several characters, and can thus preserve the sense of unfolding drama (or dramas). In other words the overall narrative interest is maintained in spite of the fact that the story edges forward at what in other genres would be an untenably slow pace.

Soaps have also developed additional strategies for suggesting that they operate to the same time-scale as that of the real world. Within the flow of other television programmes, soaps are introduced – or framed – in such a way as to create the illusion that the viewer is literally going to be conveyed to the (soap) place in question in order to catch up on all that has been happening since he or she was last there. Continuity announcements play an important part in suggesting there is a natural link between audience and soap opera worlds. A standard introduction is along the lines of: 'It's Tuesday evening, so it's time to pay a visit to Coronation Square, to see whether Jim and Joan have finally sorted out their. . . '. Similarly the opening credits of many soaps will take the form of a homing-in sequence by means of which the viewers are conveyed – via several well-known landmarks – to the familiar street, square or ranch. The accompanying signature tune also reinforces this sense of moving into a familiar world, from which we have been only temporarily absent.

A further strategy for reinforcing a sense of contemporary reality in soaps takes the form of allusions to persons or events which have a separate existence outside the fictional realm. Soaps tend to tread quite warily in making such references, since in most cases the fact that story-lines are normally planned months in advance precludes the introduction of topical references. In order, however, to create some sense of actuality, most soaps will work into the narrative occasional references to events of a seasonal nature or ones which recur at fixed points in the calendar (thus permitting maximum forward planning). Christmas or New Year parties and certain national anniversaries such as Thanksgiving Day or Guy Fawkes night are typical instances of the attempt to introduce topicality. They also have the added benefit of making it seem that a national audience is bound together in common cause or celebration.

In some cases the desire to inject actuality is taken a stage further and real life personalities are drafted in for this purpose. This is especially true of American soaps where ex-first lady Nancy Reagan and ex-President Ford have both made guest appearances in TV serials. British soaps for their part do not resort so frequently to the guest appearance device, and appearances such as those by Larry Grayson in one or two episodes of *Crossroads* were very much the exception rather than the rule. Where personalities do play a role in British soaps is when they are used in various promotional events which often involve a visit to the set where the soap is being made. This not only provides a series of photo-opportunities for the visiting political or show-biz personality, but is also one more way of enhancing the 'reality status' of the soap fiction. A recent example of this type of ploy was when in October 1989 *Coronation Street* moved to its new pattern of three episodes a week. To mark the event, the well-known TV personality Cilla Black visited the Street, chatting with characters as if they were real and speculating with them about what the future would bring.

Besides encouraging the belief that all that we are witnessing is happening in the here and now, soaps are also especially adept at establishing a strong sense of place. Even in those cases where the world evoked is in marked contrast to our own (as in, say, *Dallas* or *Dynasty*), the contours of the various settings become familiar enough to lay claim to the pseudo-reality of which we spoke earlier. With those soaps on the other hand in which a greater familiarity with the setting can already be presupposed, there can be a much stronger sense of realism. This means in effect that the nearer to home – in a social or geographical sense – the soap is, the more likely it is that strong bonds of attachment can develop. (See p. 105–7 for more on regional and national soaps.)

All soaps in one way or another will keep returning viewers to the limited number of predominantly indoor settings in which the majority of the action and dialogue will take place. Whilst most soaps will give at least some indication of a wider world beyond the immediate setting of street or square, there are a few which extend their horizons to include the surrounding district or region. This is particularly true of what we might call the 'rural soaps', of which the two best known British examples are Yorkshire Television's *Emmerdale* and Scottish Television's *Take the High Road*. These serials use the scenic splendour of the Yorkshire Dales and West Highland landscape respectively, as authentic backdrops to the everyday stories of life in a typical village community. As such the

Conveying viewers to a familiar street, *Coronation Street*

world which is evoked has very specific regional connotations, although never to the extent that local knowledge is required to fully savour the stories. Producers are keen to ensure that the elements which mark the regional origins of the programme (accents, costume, issues treated) are all integrated in a way that allows access by a wider audience. As might have been expected, however, – and as is evidenced by letters written to the respective production companies – viewers in these regions develop a particular affinity with a soap which in some measure reflects some of their concerns and captures something of their own identity. This is undoubtedly one of the main reasons why in those ITV regions where the above two programmes are made, both often achieve higher ratings than soaps which top the national ratings such as *EastEnders* or *Coronation Street*.[2]

---

2   It should also be noted here that under the terms of the franchise arrangements for the various ITV companies, it is a requirement that a certain proportion of programmes should reflect the regional identity of the area served.

What sort of real world is this?

As we have seen in the previous section, soaps like to give the impression of being up with the times, even though there are constraints on how topical they can be. Besides creating a general impression of the here and now, most soaps will wish to make some claim for contemporary relevance in terms of the social issues they broach. Just how many and what sort of issues are raised will vary from soap to soap. Looking back over the history of the genre, however, there has been a marked tendency for soap opera to be culturally and politically conservative. For this reason soaps have frequently been criticized for giving a particularly sanitized view of the world. The fear is that prolonged exposure to such material could result in viewers developing wrong-headed opinions about important social matters of the day.

As always when the topic of television's supposed influence is under discussion, there are particular anxieties about what younger viewers will make of these representations. A recent example of this has been the concern expressed over the Australian soap *Neighbours*, which has become a cult phenomenon with young viewers in many countries. Some critics allege that the bland stereotyping and the exclusion of any black or coloured character may actively encourage racist attitudes. Whilst not denying that *Neighbours* and soaps like it present at best a partial view of the real world, the charge that they can actually change people's views is much more difficult to sustain. As we discovered in the previous chapter, even allowing for the various forms of intense involvement that soaps encourage, it is unwise to make too large assumptions about medium- or long-term effects. As one critic has remarked: 'However close the reader or viewer pulls the fictive world towards him or her by endowing it with aspects of the "real world", this pull toward reality is counterbalanced by the text's fictional status. Thus its inherent and necessary unreality is preserved' (Allen, 1985, p. 40).

A further criticism levelled against soaps is that even when they do tackle important social issues, the treatment hardly ever falls outside the consensus view. In other words, soaps deliberately refrain from committing themselves to what might be seen as progressive solutions to the world's problems. They certainly could never be mistaken for examples of crusading 'agit prop' theatre. The reticence that most soaps display in these matters does mean that on occasions they appear to be stuck in some sort of time warp. For example, *Coronation Street* in its time has had to face the charge that it is nostalgically trapped in a world of yesteryear. As already remarked, however, soaps make no claim to be social documentaries, so – given their fictional status – perhaps it is inevitable that they will not so much anticipate or coincide with changes in the wider social sphere, as follow in the wake of developments already set in train. As Cantor and Pingree comment: 'Soap operas. . . help to maintain social integration and value consensus, albeit imperfectly' (1982, p. 13).

In spite of some of the reservations expressed above about how soaps deal with contemporary problems, there is in fact considerable diversity in the types of issues soaps choose to foreground. Divorce and family break-up, housing problems, unemployment and urban deprivation are just a few of the issues which soaps have worked into their story-lines in recent years. Indeed when a new soap makes its first appearance, one of the strategies it may employ to draw an audience may well be to confront directly some of the more controversial issues of the day. The boldest of the current British soaps in this respect is *Brookside*, to the extent that its producers have felt able to claim that theirs is the serial which most accurately depicts the social consequences of the Thatcherite enterprise culture.

The various claims on the part of soap producers that their programmes are going to open an audience's eyes to important contemporary realities have to be set against other factors which limit the degree of realism which can be introduced. The vast majority of soaps are part of mainstream programming and are screened at family viewing times. This – combined with the fact that they are primarily conceived as dramatic entertainments – sets limits: not so much on *what* issues can be broached as to *how* they are presented. Producers of soaps are well aware of the parameters within which they are operating, but are constantly having to ask themselves the question: How do we balance the dramatic needs of a particular scene with our obligations not to offend sections of the audience? Seasoned soap watchers may well recall some of the more notorious occasions when it has been alleged that soaps have overstepped the mark as far as the permitted level of realism was concerned, but it may be salutary to look a little further back into soap history to discover what constituted moral outrage at an earlier point. James Thurber reports amusingly on an early American radio soap *Pepper's Young Family*, where there was: 'a recurring scene in which a man and his wife were heard talking in bed – twin beds, naturally. When the man playing the husband quit, and was replaced by another actor, indignant ladies wrote in, protesting against these immoral goings on' (1949, p. 257).

Times have changed with respect to what we are permitted to witness on our screens, especially concerning the matter of sexual explicitness. (No small number of today's soaps include scenes where a couple is seen actually sharing the same bed!) This is not to say that there are any fewer determinants as to what can be shown or talked about, it is just that the nature of the determinants has changed. Broadcasting institutions which make and screen soaps will have their own guidelines and vetting procedures to ensure that standards are maintained, but most serial drama producers will practise a degree of self-censorship in these matters, thus making it unnecessary for any form of institutional intervention. Seen from a different perspective, however, it is the viewers themselves who exert a constraining influence in these matters, since audiences normally have strong ideas on what is appropriate for the soaps they so regularly patronize.

With British audiences the issue of strong language has always been an especially sensitive one, so most attempts by soap producers to give what in many ways would be a more realistic account of ordinary people's actual speech, complete with the full range of colourful phrases, has usually called forth a storm of criticism. *Brookside* in its early days, for instance, was subject to various watchdog operations, including an initiative on the part of one tabloid newspaper to produce a day-by-day 'filth count', whilst *EastEnders* after its launch in 1985 was also closely monitored for similar transgressions. In the case of *Brookside*, however, the welter of negative press criticism was accompanied by a significant fall in audience ratings. This led the programme's producers to tone things down somewhat, or as those involved in producing the programme put it: 'to smooth away its initial rough edges' (Redmond, 1987, p. 107). With *Coronation Street* the relationship between the programme and its audience is one that has been built up over a much longer period. The unwritten rules governing what can be heard and seen are therefore that much more binding. On the subject of language the producers have a very clearly formulated policy: 'We don't have any swearing. It just does not and will not happen. Characters do say 'bloody' from time to time. But even then it has to be a pretty extreme situation.' (David Liddiment quoted by John Millar in the *Daily Record*, 21 November 1989.)

Realism and artifice

In this chapter we have had occasion to comment on the various strategies employed in soaps to create or heighten the realism of the programme in question. What is being suggested is that in order to create the illusion of reality a considerable measure of artifice is employed. The artifice involves the use of a whole series of techniques which have evolved in the course of the genre's development, including both the way in which the narrative is structured

Rural realism: Scotland's nastiest soap star in *Take the High Road*

and the fashioning of an appropriate televisual style. Expressed in slightly different terms, audiences will judge how realistic or true-to-life a soap is according to how closely it conforms to the style or mode of presentation they have come to accept as realist.

In assessing the features which contribute to the 'realism' effect in soaps, one cannot underestimate the importance of certain conventions in fostering the illusion of realism. As far as their visual rhetoric is concerned, most traditional soaps will adopt a style that aims for the greatest possible transparency. This means that they cultivate a style which does not draw attention to itself, but draws viewers into the fiction as if they were unobtrusive observers of the action, witnessing events as if they were real. The techniques by which such effects are achieved have much in common with – and are in part derived from – certain classic Hollywood film practices, which also attempt to create the illusion of a seamless flow of events (see also Allen, 1985, pp. 64–7). The predominance of certain types of shot (mainly medium close-up or close-up) has in itself become an accepted part of the visual rhetoric of traditional soaps, as has the fairly restricted range of movements the camera is allowed to indulge in. By the same token the actual sequencing and duration of shots, together with techniques for switching between shots, also tends to conform to certain well-established patterns or practices.

Standard domestic situations, for instance, – among the most frequent scenes in any soap opera – will usually be filmed in medium close-up using alternating shots of the protagonists, with the occasional longer shot for the sake of variation and as an aid to viewer orientation.

Of all the camera shots which have become associated with the visual language of soaps, one of the most familiar is the close-up reaction shot. This is the shot which is often used to close an episode, the audience being left to dwell upon all the implications of the news or event which has so stunned, exhilarated or perplexed the character in question. Close-up reaction shots – whenever they occur – heighten the viewer's sense of sharing in the character's emotional response. And because it is often the case that we are well acquainted with this person, the look almost invariably carries with it a set of other associations or memories.

Like all other stylistic conventions, the full-face reaction shot works because it has been accepted by audiences as suited to the type of stories soaps tell. As we have seen, soaps concentrate mainly on dialogue and on characters' responses to events and situations rather than fast-moving action sequences. Audiences have become fully adjusted to this mode of presentation, so the degree of realism they are willing to accord to a serial depends on the extent to which the programme falls in line with these expectations. Even minor deviations from the standard techniques can result in the programme forfeiting something of its credibility. This does not mean to say that changes cannot be introduced over a period of time. The gradual phasing in of more material shot on location clearly disproves this. What producers and directors of soaps are wary of, however, is introducing these changes too quickly, for this could have the undesirable effect of drawing attention to the technical means by which the illusion of reality is created.

Soap parodies

Exposing the considerable artifice that goes into the making of soaps has been one of the major aims of this book. It has, among other things, involved looking at how they are constructed and what conventions they rely upon to achieve some of their most characteristic effects (including that of realism). One of the best ways of gaining increased awareness of the more formulaic aspects of soap opera design is to consider the various parodies of the genre. A parody of a soap – by exaggerating certain of the standard generic conventions – aims to create comical and satirical effects.

Because soaps have entered the cultural consciousness in the way they have, they are frequently the subject of jokes, cartoons or TV

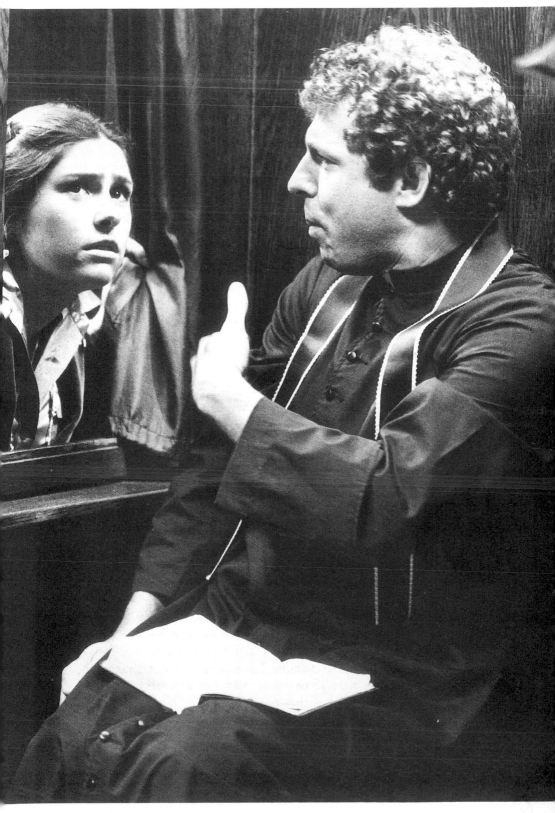

The America drama serial *Soap*

comedy sketches. There have also, over the years, been several examples of whole programmes which use (or should it be abuse?) the serial format. The best known of these are the American productions *Soap* and *Mary Hartman, Mary Hartman*, both of which systematically reduce to near absurdity many of the standard soap ingredients which were already apt to stretch credibility. Besides parodying the narrative conventions of the genre, the programmes in question also specifically draw attention to certain real-life issues, for instance religion and politics, which the normal daytime soaps have tended studiously to avoid. As might have been anticipated, these parodies have not been universally popular and in some cases appear to have earned the healthy disrespect of long-term soap watchers. This is not, one imagines, so much because the programmes have offended by introducing certain taboo subjects, but more because they deliberately set out to reveal the mechanisms by which the illusory reality of soaps is created.

If soap parodies highlight the degree to which soaps depend for their effect on observing a series of conventions, they also tell us something about the way in which audiences make sense of drama serials. For a parody to be successful, it has to focus attention on certain general and recurrent characteristics of soaps, which audiences recognize as such. In other words, viewers are being asked to draw on the knowledge that they have built up by watching several different soaps over a period of years. This allows us to make a final point about the reality status of soaps: that – in common with other fictional texts – television soaps are made meaningful primarily by relating them to other television fictions and not to any known external reality. (The term 'intertextuality' is sometimes used to describe this approach to the reception of texts.) The contention is that reality cannot be accessed directly and that meanings can therefore only be made by connecting up the 'present' text with the large number of texts like it already in circulation. Expressed more simply, when we sit down to watch a new soap, we bring with us the sum total of all our former soap-watching experience and will use this in negotiating a meaning from what we see and hear.

Concluding remarks

In view of some of the points raised in the course of this chapter, the question: 'How real are soaps' is possibly more problematical than it may have first appeared. What is indisputable, however, is that there is considerable variation in the level of reality that individual viewers are willing to attribute to the soaps which they watch. For many in the audience the serials will bring constant reminders of the world they inhabit on a day-to-day basis, and will prompt questions as to what they would do faced with similar problems to the soap characters. Other viewers, in contrast, adopt what one might term a critically quizzical attitude to the soap entertainment and are not to be persuaded that the on-screen events have anything but the most tenuous link with the real world. To illustrate just how far apart viewers can be in their response to the same programme, consider the following statements of two viewers of the popular British soap *EastEnders*:

EastEnders is as interesting as ever. It points up the problems faced by blacks, lesbians, gays and women in a very positive way and puts them in context, so that you feel you can understand and identify with the problems and pressures yourself.
[Local Government Officer, Brighton] (Day-Lewis, 1989, p. 275).

Being East Enders ourselves we do watch at 7.30 p.m. tonight. But this programme is as far removed from our type of East End environment as a Martian entering our orbit. It is dull, depressing, full of whingeing and whining characters. They have none of the true East End grit and character . . .
[A viewer in London E16] (ibid. p. 273).

6 Soap international

To say that soaps have come a long way since their beginnings as daytime radio serials in the early 1930s would be a considerable understatement. Not only do they now command huge national audiences (in Britain they have for several years been the most popular form of television programming), they have also for some considerable time been travelling the world. In an increasingly competitive audio-visual market place and with the rapid growth in television channels, we can probably also anticipate an even brisker trade in the buying and selling of TV drama serials in the years to come. This will doubtless give rise to a further chorus of critical dissent, in terms that argue that cheap, bought-in foreign soaps together with the equally ubiquitous game shows are the biggest threat to quality television.

The aim of the present chapter is to consider TV drama serials as an international phenomenon. We shall be looking at the question from a number of different perspectives, including some of the economic issues which are raised by this trading in television fictions. Limitations of space will mean that we will only be able to explore certain general trends, but we shall also be examining two or three of the most conspicuous individual international successes. It is well known that certain soaps (e.g. *Dallas*) have had an impact which appears to go beyond that of simple dramatic entertainment and that they have acquired a global reputation. This has led to concern being expressed in some quarters that countries may be laying themselves open to undesirable cultural infiltration and to the demand that more rigorous import restrictions should be imposed to resist the foreign invasion. An alternative response to the economic or cultural threat that imported soaps are sometimes perceived to represent is a more vigorous support for home-grown products. It has, however, sometimes been difficult to persuade television companies of the virtues of such a strategy since the costs of acquiring imported soaps are so much less than producing one's own. In Britain, for instance, the costs of buying in Australian or American soaps are generally considered to be five to ten times less than the cost of home-produced serial drama.

The advantages of becoming a home-producer are not just to be measured in terms of the diminished reliance on imports. It also makes you into a potential exporter. America, as the world's chief exporter of television material, has continued to play a leading role as supplier of soaps to the world, but other national producers are beginning to emerge. British and Australian programme-makers have for some time now been marketing their wares internationally, whilst in the last few years Brazil too — with its 'telenovelas' — has become a major exporter. In those cases where the costs of programme production have been partly, or even wholly, recouped from the home market, the material can be offered to foreign buyers at extremely competitive prices, thus making it more likely that it will be acquired.

Extending the outreach

The international success of the American supersoaps *Dallas* and *Dynasty* has tended to disguise the fact that soaps have always travelled, even inland. Export sales to near or distant lands are, however, just one of the ways in which a serial can gain a larger and wider audience. An equally important role in extending the outreach of serials has been through the various types of network arrangement which have developed over the years. In the early days of radio in the United States, for instance, the emergence of two or three leading network organizations meant that radio soaps were soon reaching a large nationwide audience. Similarly, the dozen or so most popular American daytime TV soaps generate very large audiences by being broadcast on the major networks.

In Britain networking has operated on slightly different lines, but the objective — that of maximizing the available audience — has remained the same. All the long-running home-produced TV drama serials currently being shown on the ITV network, for instance, started out life as 'regional' soaps made by one of the ITV companies. To secure their long-term future, however, these serials have needed to gain and maintain access to the wider audience the network provides. *Emmerdale*, for instance, the rural drama serial started in 1972 by Yorkshire Television, first occupied a lunchtime slot in the Yorkshire region. By 1975 it was being shown in most ITV regions — still at lunchtime; but by the late 1970s it had graduated to a twice-weekly nationwide showing at peak-viewing time, where it has since remained. With *Take the High Road*, the drama serial put out by Scottish Television, it is a similar story. Started in 1979, the programme quickly found favour with Scottish audiences, but in the course of the 1980s it began to be shown in the other regions belonging to the ITV network (although not, incidentally, in the same early evening slot it occupies in Scotland).

If a soap succeeds in getting networked and thereby gains access to a large national audience, it also considerably enhances its chances of further extending its outreach via export sales. Britain's longest-running soap *Coronation Street*, for instance, which was launched in December 1960, was very quickly taken up by the ITV network and soon was being enjoyed all over the country. Within a few years it had acquired the status of a national institution which it still retains today. Having attained this level of popularity, it was also not long before the serial began attracting the attention of international programme buyers. It has for many years now been regularly transmitted in many different parts of the world, although one subject of much conjecture has been how some of the programme's more colourful Northern expressions have been rendered – via subtitling or dubbing – in some of the countries where it has been screened!

As might have been anticipated, the reactions to imported serials – measured in terms of audience ratings and viewer response – have differed, sometimes quite sharply, from country to country. A number of factors will determine how well an incoming programme is received, but much will depend on whether viewers are already conversant with that particular type of serial drama and on how much understanding is required of the particular cultural setting of the soap in question.

For these reasons it should come as no surprise to learn that such an archetypically British soap as *Coronation Street* quickly built a sizeable audience when it was screened in Australia, Canada and New Zealand. Long-standing cultural ties and familiarity (partly through other film and television productions) with the social world being evoked, meant that viewers could feel relatively at home with the settings and the subject matter. In the United States on the other hand, *Coronation Street* – at least initially – did not prove to have the same appeal. One of the additional reasons sometimes advanced to explain this relative lack of appeal is that the soaps with which Americans are most familiar bear little resemblance to many British soaps with their greater emphasis on social realism. This – together with some of the linguistic challenges posed by 'Street' dialogue and the super-abundance of home-grown American soaps – has meant that *Coronation Street* has not been able to capture the large audiences in the United States that it has elsewhere.

With one of the more recent British drama serials, *EastEnders*, launched by the BBC in February 1985, it has been a very similar story. The programme has gone down well in Canada, New Zealand and Australia, for some of the same reasons, one presumes, as *Coronation Street*. *EastEnders* has also been screened in Norway, Denmark, Holland, Belgium, the Basque country and Catalonia (where incidentally it is dubbed into Catalan – a triumph indeed of the dubber's craft!). In the United States the programme, after a slow start, has since been acquired by 21 of the small public-television stations and is apparently enjoying something of a cult following throughout the country.

It is claimed however that viewers still have occasional problems with the characters' 'insular slang and serrated diction', but subscribers to the stations screening the programme can receive a special *EastEnders* glossary to help them with more unfamiliar expressions (Wolcott, 1989, p. 26). One factor which may have prevented it from becoming even more popular in the United States may be linked with the show's particular dramatic style. As one observer has noted: 'There is an innate conservatism in US television . . . and introducing a new product is always a tremendous risk. Furthermore, "realistic" soaps like *EastEnders* represent a fairly unfamiliar genre. The American daytime soaps may be more moth-eaten than *Dynasty*, but they are still more glamorous than any British equivalents' (Reisz, 1986, p. 29).

International trading

The international popularity of the soap opera format and the voracious appetite of television stations all over the world for schedule-filling material has – as suggested – resulted in soaps becoming part of a multi-million pound export trade. For programme producers and for the companies handling sales and distribution, trading in television soaps can be a very lucrative business. Moreover, as the costs of TV drama production escalate, the possibility of being able to find international buyers for one's product are beginning to play an increasingly important role in the economic calculations of would-be producers. When launching *EastEnders* for instance, the BBC was confident that the programme would be able to capitalize on the BBC's reputation for quality drama – whether of the traditional costume-drama variety or for major series such as *Edge of Darkness*. As far as the BBC is concerned, worldwide sales of a programme like *EastEnders* not only help recoup the high production costs but also enhance its reputation as an institution eager to generate a higher proportion of its income from programme sales.

In terms of international trading, however, the economic advantages always lie with those producers who have initial access to a large national audience. For if you succeed in recovering most of your production costs from home sales, you can then afford to offer your wares on the international market at extremely competitive rates. As already suggested (see p. 104–5) this is one of the reasons for the worldwide success of the American supersoaps, for whose producers the overseas sales represented very much the 'icing on the cake' in the form of enhanced profit margins for a product which had proved economically viable on the strength of home sales alone. However, if a programme displays too many exotic or foreign traits, it is likely to encounter consumer resistance. In other words: to find a measure of acceptance with an audience, imported soaps have to be identifiably different from the better-known home-produced programme but not fall too far out of line with expectations about a certain form of television entertainment. On the other hand, where there are no domestic equivalents of a particular type of foreign serial, this may well enhance its appeal (see Lealand, 1974, p. 94).

In those countries where there is a particularly strong tradition of home-produced serials, imported soaps will generally find it more difficult to capture a substantial number of viewers. In Brazil, the relatively poor showing of *Dallas* in the national ratings may well be explained by the plentiful supply of home-produced drama serials known as 'telenovelas'. It is no exaggeration to say that 'telenovelas' had, by the late 1970s, become the single most important category in Brazilian television production (Straubhaar, 1988, p. 59) and that these had quickly found favour with large sections of the television audience. One of the reasons for the rise of the 'telenovela' industry back in the early 1970s, however, had been that broadcasters and politicians felt that – given the then fragile state of the Brazilian economy – they should reduce their dependence on what were for them expensive imports. Hence the big drive to promote indigenous production, a move which has proved so successful that Brazil now finds itself exporting 'telenovelas' to television organizations throughout the world. A further consequence has been that for large numbers of Brazilian viewers 'telenovelas' quickly became a part of the staple diet of television entertainment, so much so that even *Dallas* was not able to make the sort of impact it did in other countries.

The Dallas phenomenon

In the case of Brazil the flourishing 'telenovelas' industry, which has incidentally been virtually monopolized by one producer, namely *TV Globo*, has been successful enough to forestall incursions by foreign competition. In other countries, one of the recurrent concerns has been that over-dependence on foreign imports would pose a threat to existing domestic production. This in turn has led in many cases to the introduction of various types of quota system to govern the inflow of such material. The reasons for such steps being taken are, however, only partly economic. It also has to do with a nagging fear about what sort of impact the imported programme

Soaps from Brazil: *Malu Muller*

will have on the viewers themselves, if they are exposed to material which may reflect very different values and concerns to those which have traditionally found favour in their own culture.

The type of threat these programmes supposedly represent is often referred to as cultural imperialism, and this has been the subject of much earnest debate. At a UN conference in 1982, for instance, Jack Lang, the French Minister for Culture, had fighting words to say about 'a financial and intellectual imperialism that no longer or rarely grabs territory but grabs consciousness, ways of thinking, ways of being' (Billson, 1987). Because of their undisputed popularity with viewers in many countries, American series and serials have been the particular butt of criticism in this respect. In the early 1980s when *Dallas* was proving such an international success, the spectre of 'wall-to-wall *Dallas*' was raised, suggesting that national broadcasters would soon no longer be able to defend themselves against a flood of unwanted imports.[1]

---

1   It is interesting to note that the scorn poured on foreign soaps tends to be loudest at times when major changes in the organization of broadcasting are being considered. In Britain in the early 1980s the introduction of cable television led to fears of this type (wall-to-wall *Dallas*), whilst in the late 1980s plans for the progressive deregulation of broadcasting resulted in more worries about schedules becoming saturated with game-shows and foreign soaps.

This negative response to imported television serials takes a variety of forms ranging from a mild apprehension about exposure to alien value systems, to the passionately held conviction that soaps like *Dallas* are actively contributing to a country's moral decline. There are many instances one might cite where *Dallas* in particular has been cast in this scapegoat role, but one might point to the following example as representing a general trend.

In Ireland in the early 1980s there had been an often heated debates on the issue of abortion and much concern had been expressed about the 'decline in traditional values' which had allegedly led to a spate of teenage pregnancies. In the search for causal influences, certain commentators claimed to trace a direct link between the 'bed-hopping soaps' in the *Dallas* mould and the moral abandonment which appeared to be so much in evidence throughout the land. As other critics observed at the time, however, attributing guilt in this way tended all too conveniently to off-load responsibility on to foreign influences and not to allow for other contributory factors. For one thing, one did not need to look any further than the home-produced and regularly screened Irish soaps to discover all manner of material well calculated to corrupt and deprave. As one journalist put it at the time: '. . . between *Glenroe*, *The Riordans* and *Bracken* [all well-known Irish TV soaps] every form of vice reasonably imaginable has been screened. We've had extra-marital sex, adultery, drunkenness, pub brawls: hardly the sort of stuff to improve the moral fibre' (cited in McLoone and MacMahon, 1984, p. 48).

What those observers who continue to issue dire warnings about the unfortunate consequences of over-dependence on imported soaps tend to overlook is that the actual response of viewers to such material varies considerably. As research has shown, audiences are not always as gullible or malleable as those who fear the impact of cultural imperialism would have us believe. As one critic put it very succinctly: '(American) television exporters may be imperialists . . . but the natives are not always subdued or compliant' (Lealand, 1984, p. 93). This is nowhere better illustrated than by the fact that when audiences are given the choice of watching a good quality home-produced drama serial and a frequently more glossy import, the majority of the audience will almost always plump for the domestic production.

On the other hand, it cannot be denied that programmes like *Dallas* have had an impact that has not been matched by other types of TV entertainment made in the United States. To what can one attribute this extraordinary success? For a start, viewers must have been able, among other things, to derive a range of pleasures from

Dallas and some of the other American supersoaps, which were not being provided by their own home-produced serials. There has been much speculation on the specific nature of *Dallas*'s worldwide appeal and a number of explanations as to what audience entertainment needs were being met by the continuing Southfork sagas. Of the various explanations offered, the following are those most frequently advanced. First, and perhaps foremost, *Dallas* is not cast in the traditional mould of American daytime soaps, but is made for a prime-time audience. Production values are therefore altogether more lavish, with the result that the programmes have the slickness we have come to associate with high-budget Hollywood entertainment. In other words, right from the outset *Dallas* was destined for the international market. The producers knew that viewers all over the world were already familiar with a range of Hollywood-type film and television products and thus in one sense there was a ready-made audience. The glossiness, however, does not just extend to the production values but to the whole world which *Dallas* evokes. Beautiful women and bronzed business tycoons move about in luxurious settings which some have seen as the ultimate accolade to capitalist enterprise (and which you can love or hate according to your disposition). Likewise there is far more action and physical movement than you would encounter in the traditional soaps, which have − in the words of one critic − 'always kept their radio-like character . . . in which the visual element is kept to a minimum (very sparse locations, very simple camera work, etc.)' (Ang, 1982, p. 55). The element of melodrama which many would see as a standard ingredient of all soaps is very much to the fore in *Dallas* and the other supersoaps, and many of the story-lines take viewers far beyond the cosier but more credible world of daytime or traditional soaps.

The undeniable attractions of *Dallas* for audiences abroad has, as suggested, led to the voicing of some concern that viewers would succumb to its siren-like charms only at a certain cost. When you actually examine what viewers in other countries have to say about the programme, however, it becomes clear that the range of response is far wider than those who wish to apply various forms of censorship and control would have us believe. You certainly do not have to share the value system which *Dallas* and *Dynasty* represent to gain enjoyment from watching them. You may − as many viewers claim to have done − experience considerable exhilaration at the 'sheer artistry' of it all, but otherwise feel little inclination to identify with characters who are literally worlds apart from your own experience (see Ang, 1982, p. 96). Alternatively, as someone living in a country which does not enjoy the same material benefits which are so conspicuously on display in the American supersoaps, you may even feel more than a degree of satisfaction knowing that the world of the super-rich is so evidently rent with divisions, traumas and unhappiness!

Euro-soap

The new age of television in the 1990s means among other things that viewers – if they are prepared to pay the price – will have a vastly increased number of channels and services to choose from. This, together with the move towards the progressive deregulation of broadcasting, has prompted fears amongst many involved in audio-visual production in Europe that there will be a new invasion of cheap – and very probably nasty – foreign (non-European) imports. The possibility has been discussed – by the European Commission among other bodies – of various ways of meeting this challenge, not so much by imposing new import restrictions as by facilitating cross-frontier broadcasting and by encouraging the production of certain types of programme material which would find favour with a large, pan-European audience.

Mindful of the success of the American supersoaps, European TV producers have been working hard in the last few years to come up with programmes which would out-Dallas *Dallas*. Such Euro-soaps would aspire to the same glossy production standards as the American supersoaps, but transfer the scenes of action to more familiar European settings. There are of course sound economic reasons for encouraging this type of European enterprise. It can provide a valuable fillip to the European media industries and give them the potential to operate in similar conditions to their American counterparts.

Ideas have been mooted for various types of Euro-soap, although so far only a few such programmes have actually reached our screens. For some years, for instance, there was talk of producing an updated, Europeanized version of the 1960s BBC soap *Compact* which was about the lives and loves of staff producing a women's magazine. The new programme was to be called *Impact* but the offices would be in Brussels or Paris, and there would be a 'multi-European cast, lots of location shooting all over the Continent and in the UK, and versions in several different languages shot simultaneously' (Dunkley, 1987). A similar Euro-soap which has been in the offing for some time has the working title *Vintage*. It is a French-British co-production and the plot is said to revolve around two families, one British, one French, involved in the cut-throat business of wine making (Coen, 1987).

Chateauvallon, the French soap designed to out-Dallas *Dallas* (shown on Channel 4)

Even if *Impact* and *Vintage* do eventually reach our screens, one cannot be very optimistic about their chances of reaching a genuinely pan-European audience. The two much-hyped, high budget Euro-soaps which have been made to date have both been conspicuously unsuccessful at attracting the attention of a larger European audience. The first of these to surface was *Chateauvallon*, a co-production made with the support of companies from France, Italy, Luxemburg and Switzerland. When it was shown in France in 1986, the programme – which very soon received the nickname 'Dallas-sur-Loire' – got high ratings (35% of the available audience) and enjoyed something of a cult success. Most of the Dallas ingredients were there, including plots which centred on bitter, inter-family rivalry, on power politics and on sexual intrigue; but French audiences were clearly won over by this home-based supersoap.

When *Châteauvallon* was shown elsewhere in Europe it proved to have far less pulling power, in spite of what was considered to be one of the most daring opening credit sequences ever witnessed on prime-time television. The reasons most frequently advanced for fellow Europeans' comparative lack of interest are two-fold. Firstly, receiving the programme in dubbed or subtitled form proved much more of a disincentive than might have been imagined. In Britain audiences had a choice of watching a dubbed or a subtitled version on different evenings; and although twice as many viewers opted for dubbing, there were constant complaints about enjoyment being impaired. Indeed the programme soon became a favourite target for ridicule on this score. A second – and possibly more serious criticism – was that *Châteauvallon* was considered by many to be not much more than a rather contrived imitation of the well-known original on which it was based. To some observers it seemed almost as if a computer had been fed with individual pieces of *Dallas* and *Dynasty* which it had then converted into a Gallic clone.

With the West German production *The Black Forest Clinic* it was a very similar story. Screened first in West Germany in 1986, this expensive co-production (made by Polyphon and commissioned by ZDF, a German television channel, and ORF, the Austrian Broadcasting Company) was also clearly modelled on its American forebears. Set in a hospital clinic and making fullest use of the beautiful surrounding countryside for extended location work, the programme drew regular home audiences of 25 million viewers per episode (60% of the total available audience). When exported to other European countries, however, the programme failed to make anything like the same impression. Problems of language transfer

Scene from the West German production *The Black Forest Clinic* (shown on Channel 4)

were again partly responsible, but for many viewers it brought too many echoes of what they already knew to command their regular attention. Foreign audiences clearly preferred their home-grown medical soaps to what they evidently regarded as a somewhat hybrid if not homogenized concoction.

On the strength of the admittedly limited experience gathered to date therefore, one can make the following interim judgement: Euro-soaps, although going down very well in their country of origin, have been much less successful when shown abroad. The attempt to graft on to 'European' stories and settings a series of *Dallas*-like features in order to appeal to a Europe-wide audience has not had the hoped-for success.

The success of the Australian soaps

From all that we have had to say about 'travelling' soaps, it should be clear that there is no one single key to worldwide success, yet certain factors do make it more likely that one soap will be better received in foreign parts than others. The following section considers some of these factors, mainly – although not exclusively – in relationship to Australian soaps, many of which have in recent years become international best-sellers.

One question which will always be uppermost in the minds of programme buyers responsible for acquiring foreign drama serials is whether the programme on offer will provide an attractive alternative or addition to soaps currently being shown. In the case of those American soaps imported into Britain the emphasis on fantasy and the fast-moving narratives are obviously seen as a useful counterbalance to the more gritty realism of many of the home-produced soaps. This would also explain why the American daytime serials which are far less flamboyant in style and approach than their prime-time counterparts have generally not been exported on anything like the same scale (see Lealand, 1984, pp. 80–82).

For many viewers one of the particular attractions afforded by imported soaps is the access they provide to different settings and lifestyles. As one respondent to a questionnaire surveying the appeal of *Dallas* put it: 'Sometimes I enjoy watching a different way of life, with different standards and more outspokenness. They seem to have less constraint than we have' (Lealand, 1984, p. 80). Some of these 'lifestyle' attractions are to be found in the new wave of Australian soaps, many of which emanate from the studios of the Grundy Organisation. Soaps like *Neighbours* and *Home and Away* have not only done well in Australia; they have also succeeded in attracting large followings throughout the world. In Britain, there were weeks during 1989 and early 1990 when *Neighbours* came very close to dislodging *EastEnders* and *Coronation Street* from their top position in the BARB (Broadcasters Audience Research Board) television ratings.

The phenomenal impact of *Neighbours* cannot, however, just be explained by the 'lifestyle' attractions it affords, so it is worth looking a little more closely at what else contributes to its widespread appeal. As with other products which have come to enjoy international acclaim, the secret of its success appears to have a lot to do with the application of a carefully worked-out formula which includes many of the standard generic components but also introduces one or two special features. Principal among these is the element of youth appeal. Until the arrival of *Neighbours* younger viewers had by and large not been particularly well served by television soaps. So by creating a serial which was so obviously targeted at the younger generation, the producers of *Neighbours* immediately gained access to a previously untapped audience – both nationally and internationally.[2]

As is often the case with programmes which become phenomenally successful, the initial prospects for *Neighbours* were not exactly encouraging. When it was first shown on Australian TV's Channel 7, its ratings were poor. One of the explanations offered was that it was overly concerned with social issues. It did no better when it was taken over by the Sydney-based Channel 10 in January 1986 and this led to the programme being put on four weeks' notice. At this point a determined, last-ditch attempt was made to revive the serial's failing fortunes by injecting those elements calculated to enhance its appeal to a more youthful audience. After a major restyling exercise and a vigorous promotional campaign, the fortunes of the programme began to change, and by autumn of that year *Neighbours* was being watched by almost a third of the total Australian population, many of them doubtless lured by front-page newspaper headlines such as 'Teen Love Scenes To Shock Viewers'. By the middle of 1989 *Neighbours* had clocked up more than 1,000 episodes and had an international audience of more than 30 million people in 12 different countries. As one TV journalist put it at the time: '*Neighbours* guarantees ratings as surely as the royal family sells magazines' (Toner, 1989).

---

2 A similar phenomenon could be observed in the early 1980s when the American drama series *Fame* became a cult success with younger audiences throughout Europe. As critics remarked at the time, part of the programme's appeal was attributable to there being no real European equivalents (see Lealand, 1984, p. 25).

In Britain the arrival of another Australian soap (in October 1986) did not at first create too much of a stir. After all, daytime TV audiences were already familiar with a variety of Australian serials ranging from *The Sullivans, Sons and Daughters*, and *A Country Practice* to *The Young Doctors* (a much maligned medical soap which with the passing years had come to be seen as more and more of a parody of the soap opera format). *Neighbours* was initially scheduled to be shown at lunchtime, with a repeat showing early the following morning, but its rapidly increasing popularity with the younger generation soon earned it an early evening slot in the BBC 1 schedule.

The secret of *Neighbours'* success undoubtedly has much to do with the contrast it affords with the grittier realism of many home-grown soaps. *Neighbours* is a bright, upbeat product and has quite a rich vein of humour running through it. Also, whereas British soaps have traditionally confined themselves to an interior world – sometimes creating a rather cramped and claustrophobic effect – *Neighbours* revels in the sunshine and space of the great Australian outdoors. This in turn enables there to be a continuing celebration of 'the body beautiful', a trait which has certainly done nothing to diminish the programme's ratings both at home and abroad!

Predictably enough, there has been concern expressed in some quarters about the gulf between the world of *Neighbours* and the known realities of Australian life. As Germaine Greer once fulminated: 'The world of *Neighbours* is the world of the detergent commercial . . . Everyone's hair and underwear is freshly laundered. No one is shabby or eccentric; no one is poor or any colour but white.' (*Radio Times*, 11–17 March 1989.) For the international television audience, however, it seems unlikely that the squeaky clean, all too homogeneous society of *Neighbours* will be mistaken for a documentary representation of contemporary Australia. The pleasures of watching the serial are of a different order, and at least part of the attraction is that the world projected has something of the quality of a dream. But whereas the American dream pays homage to fast cars, palatial buildings and vast riches, the Australian version emphasizes the cultivation of a particularly carefree, outdoor lifestyle in an untroubled environment which seems at times hermetically sealed off from the real world.

For Germaine Greer all this adds up to a dangerous distortion of important social realities, but that only represents one way of looking at the programme. Another would be to suggest that *Neighbours* has taken some of the more familiar ingredients of soap opera – melodramatic, family-centred stories and a well-defined community setting – and forged them into a serial which combines some of the

qualities of the more glitzy American supersoaps with those of the more down-to-earth British serials, where slice-of-life realism is almost always tempered with various forms of humorous relief. As one critic has observed: '*Neighbours* has the sense to punctuate melodramatic excess with character comedy; its narratives are rich and involving, but they never browbeat or hector' (Medhurst, 'The Australian for saga', *The Listener*, 31 December 1987, p. 26).

Prospects for the future

With the demand for television entertainment growing as it is, there seems no reason to suppose that the international market for popular drama serials will do anything but expand. It is also likely that in the foreseeable future those countries which have acquired knowledge and expertise in producing this kind of drama will continue to hold a dominant position as the major programme providers. In the medium term, however, as certain channels begin to cater for the tastes of different sorts of audience, it is possible that viewers will be able to choose from a greater range of imported material from a variety of national sources. In Britain, for instance, since the arrival of Channel 4, the viewing public has had the opportunity of watching drama serials made not only by our European neighbours but also by producers in South America and Asia.

In contrast to other types of television programme material (with the possible exception of the television series), drama serials clearly have that much more of an international appeal. One might even go so far as to say that soaps – focused as they are on dramas which stem from people living together in family or group situations – can claim a near universality which is denied to other forms of dramatic entertainment which tend to be more culturally specific. International audiences, in other words, can relate more easily to soaps because they recognize echoes of their own lives beneath the patina of 'foreignness'. For whilst language (both verbal and non-verbal) and settings may well be unfamiliar, many of the situations and events which form the basis of soap narratives have a cross-cultural significance. For instance, family quarrels the world over will often revolve around similar issues, so viewers will have few problems in spotting the tell-tale signs of conflict. Similarly soaps tend by and large to adopt simple and straightforward story-telling devices. There are no complicated or fancy narrative techniques and most of

Soaps from Brazil: *Isaura the Slave Girl*

the generic conventions which soaps observe have also become stan-
dardized across international boundaries. These are all features
which make imported soaps relatively easy to decipher for foreign
audiences and explain the considerable impact they have had in
sometimes unexpected places.

Given the increased pressure to produce material which will
appeal to a larger international audience, there are fears in some
quarters that producers will become so obsessed with the export
potential of their product that they will attempt to tailor it to the
perceived needs of an international audience. In the words of one
concerned observer: 'The obsession with the international market
and the competition for prime-time spots could prove one more step
towards the standardisation of national programmes' (Mattelart *et
al.*, 1984, p. 104). The problem, or challenge, for producers therefore is to preserve those elements which give the programme a
specifically local feel, but not to overload it in such a way as to
create problems of accessibility for non-local audiences. Programme
makers who become nervous about the inclusion of significant local
detail run the risk of producing a serial which will be thought to be
bland and lacking in credibility. After all, one of the defining characteristics of soap opera is that the action should be rooted in a clearly
defined environment which will in some measure determine what
transactions occur between the various characters. If you remove
those significant local details in the hope of enhancing the programme's international marketability, the result may be a lifeless,
artificial construct with no real credibility.

In spite of all that we have had to say about the comparative ease
with which soaps travel, it does sometimes come as a surprise to
learn in what countries certain soaps have been most favourably
received. Certain imported programmes have already enjoyed cult
success with particular sections of the TV audience (*Prisoner Cell
Block H* in Britain or *EastEnders* in Catalonia), but what is more
difficult to explain is the wide popularity of certain soaps in countries or regions where there could not be a bigger gulf between the
world of the audience and the world which the drama in question
evokes. As an example of this one might once again cite the case of
Scotland's own TV drama serial *Take the High Road*, which is set in
a small Highland community in the west of Scotland. Of the several
countries (including Zimbabwe and Saudi Arabia) to which the
programme has been exported, one of those where it has been most
popular has been Sri Lanka. Its popularity is such that for the past
five years it has occupied a prime-time slot in the Saturday evening
schedule (one that in other countries would be taken up by *Dallas* or
Dynasty). According to a Sri Lankan television representative,

viewers apparently find it relatively easy to 'get involved with the characters', so much so that the programme has 'now become a popular conversation topic at social gatherings'.

On closer inspection, however, it could be that other factors have been involved in winning over so many local viewers. *Take the High Road* has traditionally been one of those soaps which could be relied upon to be relatively circumspect in how it dealt with sensitive issues, especially for societies where a different set of cultural or religious values obtained. So whereas the American supersoaps such as *Dallas* and *Dynasty* were – to quote the Sri Lankan official – 'always running into censor problems with the local authorities', *Take the High Road* was regarded as quite wholesome by comparison and could in this way build a large, appreciative audience. What Sri Lankan audiences will make of the recent changes to the programme which have given *Take the High Road* a more upbeat and youth-oriented image – with visits to discos, drinking and flirtation much more prominent than before – is of course a different matter entirely!

FURTHER READING

Allen, Robert C. (1983), 'On Reading Soap Operas: A Semiotic Primer' in *Regarding Television* edited by E. Ann Kaplan, pp. 97–108, Frederick, Md., University Publications of America.

*Allen, Robert C. (1985), *Speaking of Soap Operas*, Chapel Hill and London, The University of North Carolina Press.

*Ang, Ien (1985), *Watching Dallas: Soap opera and the melodramatic imagination*, London and New York, Methuen Books.

Barrett, Ellen (1985), 'Daytime soap in America', in *European Broadcasting Union Review* (Programmes, Administration, Law) Vol. XXXVI, No. 6, November, 1985, pp 37–8.

Barthes, Roland (1977), *Image-Music-Text*, Glasgow, Fontana Paperbacks.

Bichsel, Hannes (1984), '*Motel* – a low-budget series', in *European Broadcasting Union Review* (Programmes, Administration, Law), Vol. XXXV. No 6, November, 1984, pp. 13–15.

Billson, Anne (1984), 'Savon-sur-Loire', in *Time Out*, 28 January – 4 February, 1984, pp. 13–15.

*Buckingham, David (1987), *Public Secrets: EastEnders and its Audience*, London, BFI Publishing.

*Buckman, Peter (1984), *All for Love*, London, Secker and Warburg.

*Cantor, Muriel and Pingree, Suzanne (1983), *The Soap Opera*, Beverly Hills, California, Sage Publications.

Cassata, Mary and Skill, Thomas (eds.) (1983), *Life on Daytime Television Tuning-In American Serial Drama*, Norwood, New Jersey, Ablex Publishing Corporation.

Coen, Harry (1987), 'Eurosoap', in *Today* 24 January.

— Day-Lewis, Sean (1989), *One Day in the Life of Television*, London, Grafton Books.

Dunkley, Chris (1987), 'Eurosoap can't wash away *Dallas*', in *Financial Times*, 2 February, 1987.

*Dyer, Richard *et al.* (1981), *Coronation Street*, London, BFI Publishing.

*Gerahty, Christine (1991), *Women and Soap Opera: A Study of Prime-Time Soaps*, Oxford, Basil Blackwell

Greer, Germaine (1989), 'Dinkum? No, bunkum!', in *Radio Times* 11–17 March.

*Hobson, Dorothy (1982), *Crossroads: The Drama of a Soap Opera*, London, Methuen.

Kingsley, Hilary (1988), *Soap Box: The papermac guide to soap opera*, London, Macmillan Publishers.

Lealand, Geoffrey (1984), *American Television Programmes on British Screens*, London, Broadcasting Research Unit (BFI).

Liebes, Tamar and Katz, Elihu (1986), 'Patterns of Involvement in Television Fiction: A Comparative Analysis' in *European Journal of Communication* Vol. 1 (1986), pp 151–171.

— Livingstone, Sonia (1988), 'Why People Watch Soap Opera: An Analysis of the Explanations of British Viewers', in *European Journal of Communications*, Vol. 3(1988) pp. 55–80.

McLoone, Martin and MacMahon, John (eds.) (1984), *Television and Irish Society*, Dublin, RTE-IFI publication.

Mattelart, Armand; Delcourt, Xavier[n] and Mattelart, Michèle (1984) *International Image Markets: in Search of an Alternative Perspective*, London, Comedia Publishing Group.

Medhurst, Andy (1987), 'The Australian for saga', in *The Listener* 31 December, 1987, p. 36.

Modleski, Tania (1982) *Loving with a Vengeance: Mass-Produced Fantasies for Women* Hamden, Connecticut, Anchor Books.

*Morley, David (1986), *Family Television*, London, Comedia Publishing Group.

Newcomb, Horace (ed.) (1979), *Television: The Critical View* (Second edition), New York and Oxford, Oxford University Press.

Newcomb, Horace (1974), *TV: The Most Popular Art*, Garden City, New York, Anchor Books.

Nown, Graham (ed.) (1985), *Coronation Street: 25 Years (1960–1985)*, London, Ward Lock Limited in association with Granada Television.

Podmore, Bill (1984), '*Coronation Street* – the making of a hit', in *European Broadcasting Union Review* (Programmes, Administration, Law), Vol. XXXV, No. 6, November, 1984, pp. 11–13.

Redmond, Phil (1985), '*Brookside* – a socially realistic twice-weekly drama' in *European Broadcasting Union Review* (Programmes, Administration, Law) Vol. XXXVI No. 6, November, 1985, pp. 39–42.

Redmond, Phil (1987), *Brookside: The Official Companion*, London, George Weidenfeld and Nicolson, in association with The Mersey Television Company Ltd and Channel Four.

Reisz, Matthew (1986), 'Suds law and the selling of a soap', in *The Listener* 4 December, 1986, p. 29.

Root, Jane (1986), *Open the Box*, London, Comedia Publishing Group.

Smith, Julia and Holland, Tony (1987), *EastEnders: The Inside Story. . .*, London, BBC Books.

Straubhaar, Joseph (1988), 'The Reflection of the Brazilian Political Opening in the *Telenovela* (Soap Opera), 1974–85, in *Studies in Latin American Popular Culture*, Vol. 7, pp. 59–76.

Taylor, Laurie and Mullan, Bob (1987), *Uninvited Guests*, London, Hodder and Stoughton.

Thurber, James (1949), *The Beast in Me and Other Animals*, London, Hamish Hamilton.

Toner, Barbara (1989), 'Soapbox', in *Radio Times* 29 July – 4 August, 1989.

Wolcott, James (1989), 'East of London', in *Vanity Fair* (USA edition), July, 1989, pp. 26–9.

Note: Items marked with an asterisk are especially recommended for the light they throw on the soap opera phenomenon.

INDEX